FAITH IS POWER
FOR YOU

DANIEL A. POLING

FAITH

IS

POWER

FOR YOU

NEW YORK
GREENBERG : PUBLISHER

Manufactured in the United States of America
By The Haddon Craftsmen, Inc., Scranton, Pa.

Acknowledgments

I am indebted to the following for permission to use previously published material in this volume:

LIFE: *A Protestant's Faith*. Nov. 7, 1949.

THE READER'S DIGEST: *Prayer Is Power* by Alexis Carrel. March, 1941.

REDBOOK MAGAZINE: *Very Personal* by Daniel A. Poling. 1948.

FLEMING H. REVELL COMPANY: *An Adventure in Evangelism* by Daniel A. Poling. 1925.

Contents

CONTENTS

The First Answer

THIS BOOK is the story of my faith. It is the story of how one man found peace with power. It is factual and inevitably it is very personal. It is written with a sense of mission—to share with others a reality that through all the varying fortunes of life has never failed. Prayer can be your answer, as in these pages I tell you how and where it has been mine. You too may have peace with power and have it *now*.

I do not remember my first prayer, but I do remember my first answer.

My mother taught me to pray. That first prayer is back somewhere in her arms before the gray dawn of a child's memory. The first answer? It was like this:

I was a junior in college when I became the representative of my school in a state oratorical contest. On Sunday before the Friday of the contest (which we were entertaining) I developed a severe cold and on Monday should have remained in bed. By Tuesday I had a mounting fever and in the evening when the doctor came and named my trouble "grippe," I was without a voice and in black despair at the thought of failing my school on Friday night.

The despair was half-remorse because I had invited the disaster by taking an exhaustive thirty-mile bicycle ride on the preceding Saturday. Through Wednesday the fever stood high and there were further complications. That night I was semi-delirious.

Thursday morning something happened. First, I stopped my frantic regretting and began to think with a purpose. At my head and just above the wainscotting of the little room hung a wall motto—silver letters on a green card spelling out these words from the Old Testament: "There Hath Not Failed One Word Of All His Good Promise."

Perhaps I do not know what impelled me, but I do know what I did. I rolled out of bed and, on my knees, with my burning face buried in the covers that should have been over me, I prayed. After more than forty years I remember that prayer. I prayed to be ready and able to speak on Friday night. At whatever cost I asked for that. Not to win but to be there, in my place and with voice and strength enough not to let my college down. After these years I know the prayer was right.

I did not ask for anything to the detriment of any other person. I asked only that I be able to do my assigned and accepted duty and that others not be the losers because of my weakness.

I got back into bed, pulled the covers under my chin, and had the answer to that prayer for the doctor when he came. I knew that I would speak on Friday night. But

2

when I told the doctor, told him with a grin that I was going to deliver my oration the next night, he very positively gave me the negative with all the particulars. Strangely enough, what he said did not trouble me. But a few hours later when the fever broke and I went into the great sweat that dropped me into the depths, I had a finish fight with doubt.

Then I discovered what I have never since lost: that in weakness, God is a man's strength and that His strength is matured and perfected for us in our weakness. The physiologist and psychiatrist have their answers for what happened and indeed for much that this book relates. But with those answers fully evaluated, acknowledged, and appreciated, there is something more—something more that I discovered and experienced before the student oratorical contest in Dallas, Oregon.

It is this "something more" that I would share with you, because it has given me not only peace of mind and peace of soul, but because this peace is peace with power in and over every circumstance of life.

I delivered my oration. The doctor himself—after he capitulated—aided and abetted me. I did everything he advised and took everything he prescribed, including double shots of strychnine.

It was the horse-and-buggy age and I was driven to the contest. The fortunes of the drawing made me the first speaker. I came on, was letter-perfect in my delivery if wobbly in my knees, and got off the stage before taking what is called a "nose dive" now, but was just an old-fashioned collapse then. The nearest bed was in the Methodist parsonage and there I went to stay awhile.

3

You understand that winning the contest was another matter altogether. I had not asked for that. Even then I knew that such a prayer is a wrong prayer, always a wrong prayer in such a case, for it is a prayer against men who are your associates and comrades as well as your competitors. "May the best man win" should go with you when you kneel as well as when you run.

To pray for the victory over your own weakness, to pray that you will be at your best and do your best is always the right prayer. But to pray for victory without regard is always a wrong prayer. This right prayer is the prayer of Notre Dame football teams in our time when they go to mass before a game, just as it was the prayer under the goal posts at Princeton in the time of Robert E. Speer.

But why the doctor at all? Why his aid along with the strychnine if God had taken over? For me the answer to that question is found in the New Testament: "But know ye not, o, vain man, that faith without works is dead?" Here enters, I know, the conflict with a great group of sincere men and women who pray and for whom I have only high regard.

But I do not join the conflict.

I have a story to tell and it is mine. I have an experience to share and this book is the story. It is one man's humbly recited experience. It is not a debate; it is not a philosophical dissertation; and I join no argument nor do I have a part with those who condemn or even belittle others whose prayer pattern and whose faith in faith's application differ from mine.

Prayer is both universal and individual, even as God's love. Prayer is the open door for everyone, but it is also

as personal as your name on a card. It may be one word
or many words or no words at all save as words may be
thoughts unexpressed, but always the effective prayer is
"the soul's sincere desire."

You may pray with beads and a crucifix and I without,
but God is listening when His children cry. When I offered
my first prayer to a decision, I did not even sense this vast
and universal fact.

It is a long journey from Oregon to China, but it was
in Chungking many years later that this knowledge fully
came to me. In this wartime capital I spent a long morning
with the senior Chinese Abbot of the Buddhist faith. We
talked about many things, but chiefly he told me the particulars of his own belief; and then when our conference
approached its end, he turned to Jesus Christ. Not many
Christians could offer a more devout and moving "confession of faith" than this Columbia University trained
Buddhist voiced that December morning in 1943.

He was clearly conservative rather than liberal in his
theology, and Trinitarian rather than Unitarian. He accepted the Virgin Birth and the Deity, and all the mature
culture of the East flowed through the prayer he offered
for my safe return across the "Hump" to my own kin and
country.

That morning remains with me as a major spiritual
experience of my life. The serene face of the man, his
deep, far-seeing eyes, the expressive hands cuffed in spot-
less white cotton, the venerable though still vibrant body,
and the unforgettable voice that will speak to me across
the distances until my time shall end—these are all within
the memory of that prayer which began: "Our Father,

Who art in Heaven . . ." Chungking, China, and the Buddhist Abbot are a long way from Dallas, Oregon, and a college junior, but the prayers are one.

A very unusual interfaith conference preceded my personal visit to the rooms of the Abbot. At the suggestion of this eminent Chinese representative, Buddhists, Catholics, Mohammedans, and Protestants had come together and organized the four faiths in support of China and Chiang Kai-shek in the resistance movement against Japan. They gave themselves a significant name—"Believers in God." On the occasion when I met with the group, one other American, a Baptist missionary with half a century of service in China, the Papal Nuncio who was an Italian, and I were the only foreigners present.

For my benefit, since I alone did not understand the Chinese language, the conversations and talks were all in English or translated. This remarkable group of "Believers in God" was made up of both men and women who prepared releases each week for all Chinese newspapers. The material sent out was first assembled from the available sources, then digested, rewritten, and pointed toward the common cause of Freedom and Democracy in the Far East. We lunched together that day—the American Y.M.C.A. was our host and the Abbot was the gentle and vastly wise master of ceremonies.

Among those who spoke was a devout Mohammedan who, though a general of high rank on the Generalissimo's staff, was unmistakably a mystic. For my benefit he reminded us that the Mohammedan faith was not a religion of the sword, but that on occasion it had made even the sword its instrument—"even as you and I!" He said that

6

among Mohammedans there were many sects and orders even as among Buddhists, Catholics, and Protestants. Finally he told of a shrine in the Vale of Kashmir which many Mohammedans reverence as the Tomb of Jesus, for certain of the Moslem holy men teach that after the crucifixion Jesus was removed and spirited away to the north of India where, until he died at an advanced age, he lived and taught as the Master among masters. While no Jew was present on the occasion to which I have referred, Judaism was also recognized by this war-time group of "Believers in God," whose unity was not in any sense uniformity.

Each member of the group accorded to all other members the right each claimed for himself—freedom to worship the "One God" as individual conscience directed. But the Buddhist Abbot in our later meeting said, "I must be as willing to hear what you have to say and to be convinced by it as you are obligated by your faith to say it, that is," he continued, "if I am true to *my* faith which is the eternal search."

It was not difficult to pray with so wise and good a man, and his words were with me as presently I turned my face homeward and flew across oceans and continents to spend Christmas at my own fireside—a Christmas that the Buddhist Abbot helped make the most memorable of all those sacred anniversaries I have known.

7

Prayer, My Soul's Breath

Prayer has been and is my soul's breath, as indispensable to my soul as oxygen is to my body. Indeed there are times, stark moments, when the immediate life of the body may become dependent upon prayer rather than upon physical breath. Once when oxygen failed, prayer saved my body.

On the second of February, 1918, on the Western Front in France a gas alert was sounded on the Toul sector. I with a dozen other men was in a dugout Y.M.C.A. canteen which was an extension of an old French wine cellar. Behind the double gas curtains and in our English "Box Respirators" we stood for ninety minutes. It was our first experience of the kind, and coming within twenty-four hours after a major raid that had penetrated our lines deeply at that point, it found us tense and afraid. We did not know what to expect; we could only wait—

> "The hardest thing is just to wait
> This is the agonizing fate."

The sweat ran from my armpits and soon the desire to tear the mask from my face, to rush into the air outside, to breathe deeply, became all but irresistible. That night I knew terror, stark terror, as I had never known fear before. I thought of home, remembered our children—and then I prayed. And by the faith that bends around the listening God I traveled home to peace and quiet. The guns were silenced; the batteries of 77's directly behind us and firing over us were far away; and in that humid, dark, and crowded room while the earth shook, I was alone. And yet not alone, because there was a Presence there that filled the place.

My lungs that had been literally screaming for oxygen were comforted. Whatever the answer of science—and I am sure science has an answer—breath from the soul saved the body that day.

Those who stood with me there were conscious, as I was conscious, of something that came to us and made us adequate. "As are thy days so shall thy strength be" is the ancient promise that was fulfilled to us there on the Western Front.

And so from the Oregon town to Chungking in China and back to the Toul sector in France and World War I, we have traveled as we shall continue to travel in this story. But for the one who tells the story the road is always the way to Peace with Power. It winds as it journeys and it doubles back to its starting point, but always it leads forward, since it reaches from then until now and beyond.

There was nothing labored about my first prayer. I simply dropped to my knees by my bed, made my supplication, made it believing that the answer was clearly within God's will and power, believing too that the words of the motto which hung above my head applied to me. When I got back into bed, I knew that I would not let my college down; I knew absolutely that I would speak the next evening.

Do I hear you say: "To think is to be"? Yes, definitely; and to pray like that is definitely something more, more than the conquest of mind over the material, more than a boy's will matched against fever running in the blood. Prayer called in the reserves that are outside and beyond a man's body and mind. Reserves that wait always to be called and that are no respecter of persons—reserves that are available now to you.

These are the reserves that Washington called down to Valley Forge when in the snows of that incredible winter the great commander knelt and, with despair all about him and no further human aid in sight, asked of God the added might to win for freedom. These are the reserves of power that Douglas MacArthur sought and found when, landing in Australia after his escape by submarine from Corregidor, he cabled the Rector of the church in Little Rock, Arkansas, before whose altar he had been confirmed. And they are the reserves from which a boy, hard-pressed to meet his little hour (but to him so great), drew strength and healing sufficient for his need.

These reserves have been called upon by the humble as well as by the great ever since the first prayer was uttered by a frightened voice when only fear made prayer articulate or was offered by an anguished spirit before the words of any prayer had been spoken.

Before Gettysburg Abraham Lincoln prayed, and afterward he said, "I have been driven many times to my knees by the overwhelming conviction that I had nowhere else to go. My own wisdom and that of all about me seemed insufficient for that day."

My own experience in prayer convinces me that it is a weak theology and an equally immature philosophy that affirms that prayer has only a subjective benefit. That it has, to be sure, but "the child who confidently appeals to a Father in Heaven" is infinitely more scientific than theologians and others who affirm that the benefits of prayer are only or exclusively subjective.

My first answer to prayer was affirmative, my second negative; and these two prayers were not far apart. Both were in the same year and separated by less than five months. I had spent the major part of my summer vacation in the Eastern Oregon country working at The Dalles in Waso County. Late in August I was called to my parents' home by the desperate illness of a younger brother. When I saw him lying in mortal pain with the fatal grip of typhoid fever upon him, I knew what to do!

That night in a room separated from my brother's by a partition so thin that I could hear his sharp, staccato breathing, I knelt again to ask God to keep His promise that had never failed—the promise of that old wall motto. With complete assurance I began that prayer.

But now it was different, altogether different. I got nowhere. There was no promise and no peace. I seemed as one standing before a wall of stone, or a gate of brass that would not open. I became increasingly importunate. I argued and made demands. Gradually a hopelessness came upon me. First it was amazement or the shock of disillusion, then anger, and finally despair.

I wanted the life of my brother more than I desired anything else in the world. I wanted his life so much that I was ready that night—ready and eager—to pledge my own life against his recovery. But there was no answer and not the slightest intimation that I had been heard.

Would it have been possible for me to batter through that closed door? Does the promise *ask and it shall be given you* strip down to just that?

There are some who so affirm.

I do not know and if I could, I would not assume the responsibility. If finally God does not give me the keys, I shall not take them by force. I want *His* answer. Always I may have mine without going to the trouble of praying.

But I do know—and this is an experience too—not only that asking "in His name" "changes things" that otherwise would not change, but also that there have been and still are times when prayer, as Nobel prizewinner Alexis Carrel, the distinguished physicist, has written, "is the only power in the world that seems to overcome the so-called laws of nature: the occasions on which prayer has dramatically done this have been termed miracles."

I have experienced that "miracle." And to you the road is open. If it is His answer for you, "ask and it shall be given you." And if it not His answer for you, He will satisfy you with His answer even as He satisfied me.

That night I left the house and tramped beside the little river, across the bridge and into the country. I was alone now as I had never before been alone—alone, helpless, and without hope. But I would not concede defeat.

13

The issue was too appalling. This was my first real bout with death, though death had come to our house twice before.

Tired to the bone, I came back to my room and to my knees. Now the breathing beyond that partition had changed; it galloped like a horse out of control. I could not pray, but I waited there and at last in utter weariness fell asleep.

Hours had passed since I first began to beat against that door that would not open, and the dawn had come when I opened my eyes. Before I was wide awake, I had my answer; and the answer was as definite as the other answer had been, but much more vivid and compelling.

The answer was "No."

The years that have passed since that morning when prayer led me to my first unmistakable negative have not dimmed the memory of the impression that came with the answer: I was satisfied, and with the answer came Peace. It was the answer I wanted; it was my answer. There was no rebellion in me—none at all—and there was Power, power that I knew was never to leave me, power that was to companion me in sickness as in health, through war and peace, at the birth and at the dying—until now.

That morning I found the interpretation of Christ's incredible promise: "Whatsoever ye shall ask in my name, that will I do." Until that morning I had never seen those three words, *in my name*. I had read only: "Whatsoever ye shall ask, that will I do." But *in my name* now means to me literally *in my will*. As I prayed for the recovery of my brother, there was no "thy will be done" anywhere in

14

the wild and anguished cry of my heart. I was ready to settle for nothing less than "*my* will be done."

But with the answer that came after I could no longer cry out my passionate demand, came also the assurance that "No" was not only God's word to me but that it was also the answer I wanted. Yes, it was as definite and final as that. Then I would not have exchanged the "No" for "Yes."

I do not have the particulars now and many things are clouded; there are many baffling questions. Horace Bushnell once said that there are questions for which we find no answers, questions we do not have time for now, questions that we must hang up until Eternity when there will be time enough. But through the years since I listened for my brother's last breath, I have been content to wait.

It was in that morning when he died that I came to know that he had something better than I had asked for him; that, as my father said later, "our loss is his gain." Here also the details are among the clouded things, but the reality is most real. I began to see even then that this life is the beginning and not the end. That it is, as another has said, "the childhood of our immortality." Or as an unnamed poet sings it:

"They pass from work to greater work
    Who rest before their noon,
  Ah, God is very good to them,
    They do not die too soon."

But something may be added. Faith in its ultimate reaches cannot be rationalized, but an experience with my own children has helped me understand something of the quality of what the truth itself is in degree. I have watched my children when they have dropped their toys beyond their reach, and I have heard their cries of anger or frustration or sheer grief. All is lost. For them the world has tumbled in. To you the occasion is something different. You know that all is not lost, that the world for which the child laments is intact and just about all ahead. You know too that even the child's memory of the event now to it all-important will fade before the tears are dry.

And so it is, I think, as God listens to our weeping when the occasion itself is beyond our knowledge but still within His love and power.

There was an almost mystical relationship between that brother and me. He was a deep and quiet lad. I have a picture that he held in his hand one evening when he climbed into my lap as I sat studying. He did not disturb me; but as I read, laboriously he wrote, spelling out his name in block letters across the card: RUDOLPH. Then he slid down and left the picture on my desk—the picture with his name. I have it in an old trunk; I know where it is; and when the mood is on me, I go to the attic and take it in my hands and remember the long night when in vain I battered at a door that would not open, but from which at last I turned away with the answer that was better than the one I sought—the answer that brought me Peace with Power.

And There Was a Mountain

Y EARS lie between the two prayer experiences that were mine as a very young man—experiences that set the pattern for my prayer life—and a third that was entirely different and yet within the pattern. The third experience came to me after I was a grandfather.

Both of our sons followed me into the ministry and immediately after Pearl Harbor, Clark, the younger, decided to enlist as a chaplain. Earlier he had told me quite frankly that if war came he would not be able to remain aloof. "But, Dad," he said, "if I go in, I'm not going as a chaplain," and there was an unmistakable challenge in his voice.

We grinned at each other and then I replied, "Why? Are you afraid?"

That nettled him and he came back at me with an abrupt, "What do you mean by that?"

I knew that he was thinking of the more difficult and,

as he regarded them, the more dangerous situations of armed conflict. He couldn't think of himself in a softer or more protected place than some other man, or of accepting a special consideration or exemption granted a clergyman.

"Clark," I said, "you'll try to go in—if you go—where you can count for the most. That's first with you, I know. . . . Well, the chaplaincy in World War I had the highest officer casualty rate of all the services."

He narrowed his eyes. "Are you sure of that, Dad?"

"Yes, I am sure. [Later I gave him the official figures—one out of ninety-six.] As a chaplain you'll have the finest chance in the world to die. The only difference is this: you can't kill anyone. Along with the medical corps, you'll be unarmed."

We never discussed that phase of the matter again, and in a long talk before Christmas, 1941, it was our son's settled conviction that he should become a chaplain in the Army of the United States.

Clark was particularly sensitive about his elder brother's situation and wanted no invidious comparisons made. One evening he said to me, "Dad, you must be very considerate of Daniel. It is harder for him to stay than it is for me to go. It takes greater courage for him to do what he is doing than it does for me to do what I am doing." That was in our last-but-one conversation before he sailed with his three fellow chaplains on the ill-fated *S.S. Dorchester*. I understood. Daniel had dreamed of the chaplaincy too, and only stern and irrevocable duty kept him out.

The particulars associated with this third prayer experience are so intimately related to Clark—so much a part

18

of him—that I cannot adequately identify them without including certain other incidents similar in character that preceded them.

It was in the boy's third year at Oakwood, the Friends preparatory school in Poughkeepsie, New York, when I received a telegram that read: "Meet me Grand Central eleven tomorrow. Very important. Don't tell Mother. I'm not going home. Love, Clark."

That was his first telegram to me and, to say the least, it left me uneasy. What kind of jam was he in? You may be sure that I was waiting at the train gate at eleven o'clock on Saturday morning.

As I remember it now, Clark was the first passenger through. He did not have the usual and characteristic smile that was always good to see. He flung his hand to my shoulders and kissed me. Men of our family have been reared in that ancient form of salutation—not a side-sweeping double-cheek affair, but the north of Europe unsanitary smacker full on the mouth.

"Let's go to the office," he said. "You didn't tell Mother?"

With a guilty feeling I nodded "Yes" to the question and we went directly to the study at Fifth Avenue and 29th Street.

As we entered, Clark turned back to shove a chair under the doorknob since there was no key. I was impressed by the gesture but hardly reassured. I sat down. He came and dropped into a chair directly across from me at the flat-top desk.

Putting his face into his cupped hands, he searched my face. I remember that moment now as one of the longest of my life. I thought of many things. What could it be that shut out his mother and home? I was a very unhappy father as I watched and waited, but one mistake I did not make: I asked no questions. I did not begin the conversation. I did something harder—I waited.

And then the boy across the desk came to life and said abruptly, "Dad, what do you know about God?"

Well, after what I had expected, not knowing what to expect, that was a relief but what a surprise!

What *did* I know about God? I am glad the question was a surprise, that it took me without warning, that I had no chance to prepare an answer—to get ready for him. For that question of a boy in one of his first great intellectual as well as emotional crises, only intuition—perhaps a father's intuition—had the answer. Whatever else my answer lacked, it was completely honest; and I know now that it was the only answer that could have satisfied our son.

"Clark," I replied, repeating his question, "what do I know *about* God? . . . Mighty little!"

That startled him. He straightened, but held my eyes as I went on: "Mighty little do I know about God, mighty little by the test of absolute knowledge—less now, perhaps, than I thought I knew when I sat where you sit! But, Clark, what I do know by the test of experience—sickness and health, sorrow and joy, death and life—what I do *know* about God changes my life."

There we began and there, after several hours, we left the great matter. But there through the years that followed we often returned.

We lunched in the city and then did what he had said he

wouldn't do—went home. Exactly why he had not wished
his mother to know about his trip, I never knew. Perhaps
he feared a conclusion of our interview that would have
made her unhappy. But that homecoming was one of the
happiest of a long series. His mother said afterwards that
even as we came into the house she knew that something
fine had happened, that something had come to us both,
bringing us closer together; and she always afterward
affirmed that our father-son relations were more intimate
and vital from that Saturday afternoon.

Just when this younger son reached his decision to become a preacher, I do not know; but I am sure that I knew
of the decision very soon after it became final. It was in
Detroit after a pre-Easter service I had addressed that we
went to lunch together, saw a movie, visited a doctor, and
then had a steak dinner. Clark had come in from Hope
College to see me, but also to visit the doctor. He was
having a great deal of trouble with the wrist he had broken
in the previous football season, and I found him now wearing a heavy leather support.

We saw the Detroit specialist together. It was apparent
then that his football days were over, for he was too light
for a line position and his strength to the team in both
tackling and passing was now a thing of the past.

I thought that his wrist and the doctor's bad news were
responsible for his unusual silences. He did little talking
until we retired. Then he began! It seemed that he would
never finish. We had a room with twin beds and only a
small night stand between us. It was late and I was ready
to sleep, but he had just begun to talk. He spared neither
subjects nor his father. Several times I was on the verge

of telling him to shut up and go to sleep, but each time I
stopped on the verge and listened, for something was there
—something still unsaid after all the saying, and something
that I knew instinctively I must wait to hear.

Gradually the boy ran down, or seemed to, and at last
he grew silent. Then I listened hardest and it came. Quietly
but so impressively that as long as I live I shall remember
the electric-like shock with which I heard him speak the
words, he opened his heart, and I saw my son as in all the
years before I had never known him. He flung his left arm
with its sound wrist across my bed. I felt his hand on my
chest, and then, calling me again as he had called me in
his childhood, I heard him say, "*Daddy*, I'm going to
preach. I've got to do it."

I was no longer sleepy or tired. Suddenly I knew that
I had always *wanted* this, even when I was sure and glad
that he would be the first lawyer of our line. I think all
fathers, whatever their worthy professions, have a sense
of fulfillment, a subtle feeling of justification, when a son
follows after.

The night came close to dawn before we went to sleep.

Two prayer experiences marked Clark's life before the
incident that is the third in this personal trilogy.

One August afternoon before he entered Yale Divinity
School, he came to me and said: "Dad, I'm going up on
Wolf Hill tonight after dinner and I'll not be back, well,
for some time. I'm taking a blanket and a canteen, and
please, Dad, don't worry about me, and keep Mother from
worrying. My return is indefinite." He grinned. "I may
stay twenty-four hours or longer, but there are some things
I want to settle, Dad, and I hope I won't be interrupted.

22

Where a Light Shines into a Valley

I T WAS during our son's first year at Yale that he and I took a walk down the abandoned ridge road that leads north from "Long House" toward the old Goodale farm where a governor of New Hampshire was born. Telegrams from him were not unusual now, and he sent one from New Haven just to be sure that he would find me at home. It read: "Most important. Must see you." At that time in his middle year he was serving the South Meriden Methodist Church as student pastor. He arrived at night and the next morning we took our walk— a walk, not a hike, for we were interested chiefly in undisturbed conversation.

He waited until we had crossed the main highway and climbed the long hill leading off to the right. We were in the deep, silent woods now and he began to talk: "Dad, an old man is dying in my parish and he wants me to say something to him. He needs me, Dad, and I haven't anything to say."

We stopped by an old stone wall and he waited. His words rang in my ears. "He needs me and I haven't anything to say." That was a large order, but at any rate the matter had been frankly stated. Clark was a young minister and this was the first time Death had come to him.

I told him of my first pastoral experience with Death —out in Ohio, when the mother of six small children left them all weeping at her bed, the youngest sitting on a pillow by her head. I had been younger than he. But the principal thing I told him was that he must have something to say before he could say, and something to give before he could give it; also I told him that since he so greatly desired to be helpful, there need be no question at all about receiving and experiencing, that here the problem for him reduced itself into "Ask and it shall be given you," that it was as simple, but as profound, as that. *And to those who read this book I say that what I promised the young man by the stone wall in New Hampshire is equally for them here and now.*

We talked that day to the heart of life's mystery, its beginning and its end in time. We agreed that day in the ancient and overgrown colonial roadway that this life is indeed but the "childhood of our immortality," and then quite naturally we knelt together in the long, dry grass among the dead leaves by the granite wall.

I left him—I knew he wished me to—and walked home alone. Later when he returned, I saw that he had followed the formula and had the answer. I knew that he would not disappoint the dying man in South Meriden; that he was going back with something to say, something to give—something that later in the short time of his ministry he said and gave to many people.

December, 1941, came quickly after our long walk and then our last long talk together in Philadelphia, but there were crowded days in between—his ordination, his call to the old First Reformed (Dutch) Church in Schenectady, New York, his marriage, the birth of his son, and the activities of an expanding, successful pastorate. There was a final visit in Boston when Betty, his wife, and "Corky," his small son, were also with us. But it was in Philadelphia that the young chaplain made a characteristic request that shaped the third prayer about which I write here and which, as no other prayer I have ever prayed, has led me to Peace with Power.

It was apparent that my son had something to say to me that he found difficulty in expressing, but after a long silence, as we sat together in my study, he came directly to the point. "Dad," he said, "I don't want you to pray for my return—that wouldn't be fair," he hastened to add. "Many will not return, and to ask God for special family favors just wouldn't be fair!" He grinned then and added, "You know I have a lot of confidence in your prayers!" He got up and came to the side of my chair. Dropping his hand on my shoulder, he became very earnest as he talked on. "Don't misunderstand me—I'm coming back all right—in spite of your high casualty rate for the chaplaincy." And he grinned again as he reminded me that he had not forgotten an earlier conversation. "I have no premonitions. *But don't pray for my return.* I

29

don't want to go away feeling that you're asking special favors for me, Dad. It would do something to me—not good." He waited then to see whether I understood. And when I nodded and he knew that I did understand, he went on to his conclusion which, as I remember the conversation now, was very wonderful. "Pray, Dad," he said, "that I shall do my duty and something more. Pray that I shall never be a coward. Pray that I shall have strength and courage and understanding of men, and especially that I shall be patient. Oh, Dad, just pray that I shall be adequate!" And he used the word that with us is the all-comprehensive word. Then he said, "That is the prayer, Dad, I want you to pray; and when I do come back, everything will be wonderful."

And that was the prayer we prayed and never any other —that he should be adequate. Sometimes I have wondered—but I have no regrets. That was the right prayer and it was answered.

On February 13, 1943, the War Department reported our son "missing in action in the North African area." Later the location was changed to "North Atlantic area" and on Monday, April 10, "missing in action" was officially changed to "lost in action." Our son was one of four chaplains of three faiths who were on the S.S. *Dorchester* which sank in iceberg waters within twenty-seven minutes after being torpedoed at 1:15 A.M. February 3, 1943. At that time the ship was within ninety miles of its Greenland destination. Of the 904 men on board (there were no women), 678 were finally reported "lost in action."

In an affidavit filed by Frank A. Benkler, Quartermaster, Merchant Marine Service, and signed by Fred Francis Bibler (Night Steward) and Juan L. Alejandro (Gun Crew Messman) appears the following: "The following incident was told by soldier survivors to crew survivors. Authenticity can be verified by the soldier survivors now in Greenland concerning the heroiç conduct of the four chaplains aboard the sinking ship—Jewish, Catholic, and Protestant. With utter disregard of self, having given away their life-jackets to four men without them, the chaplains stood hand in hand, praying to the God they served for the safety of those men who were leaving the stricken ship on all sides of them. This is the picture engraved in our minds and hearts as the ship disappeared beneath the waves."

The complete affidavit is filed in the office of the Chief of Chaplains, Washington, D.C. This and other documents with eye witness testimony constituted the evidence upon which the D.S.C. and the Purple Heart were awarded posthumously to each of the four chaplains.

Another survivor, Engineer Grady Clark of North Carolina, while convalescing in the Valley Forge Army hospital at Phoenixville, Pennsylvania, told of how, standing within "eight feet of Chaplain Poling," he witnessed the event. "The chaplains quieted panic," he said, "forced men 'frozen' on the rail in fear toward the boats or over the side, helped men adjust life-jackets, and at last gave away their own. They had no chance without life jackets." He spoke of Chaplain Poling's contagious laugh and concluded, "I swam away from the ship and turned to watch. The flares and northern lights now lighted everything. The bow came up high and she slid under. The last I saw,

31

the chaplains were up there praying for the safety of the men. They had done everything they could. I did not see them again."

Alexander D. Goode, the Jew; John P. Washington, the Roman Catholic; George L. Fox and our son, the Protestants. Four men of three faiths, joined in friendship and sharing in a holy mission, in death were not divided. Lost in action, surely they were found of God.

I was in a hotel just off Grosvenor Square in London when the nine o'clock B.B.C. newscast blared the story of a transport torpedoed and of a few survivors picked up, some "frozen at the oars"; of panic on the decks; of less than thirty minutes between the explosion of two torpedoes that blew the heart out of the ship and killed hundreds below decks; and of the sinking. But briefly the announcer told of four chaplains of three faiths who heroically did their duty, gave their own lifebelts to enlisted men and then, praying together, went down with the ship.

Later in North Africa I had the official confirmation that "missing in action" must now be revised to read finally "lost in action."

I remembered then a letter, Clark's first letter to me, written when he was seven, written in square, block letters and addressed by his mother to me in France. It reached me on the first Friday of February, 1918, found me in a dugout at Rombecourt on the Toul sector of the Western Front of another world war. That letter reads: "Dear Daddy: Gee, I wish I was where you are. Love, Clark." And it had come to pass that in exactly twenty-five years after the "war to end war," the war "to make the world safe for Democracy," had been fought and

WHERE A LIGHT SHINES INTO A VALLEY

"won," the desire of an eager little boy had been granted.

In our son's last letter are words that remind me of his request when we talked together in my Philadelphia study: "Apparently I am headed for a blind alley [Greenland]," he wrote, "but, Dad, if when I get there I find one other man, then there will be three of us." And in that was the haunting spirit of something Clark once wrote from prep school after he had listened to an address delivered by a medical missionary from the Sudan country in Africa. It was his first expression of the kind, the first of his religious statements: "Now I know that I could follow Jesus to the death," he wrote.

Dean Weigle of Yale, in writing to me after the *Dorchester* sinking, quoted from a confidential letter written by one of Clark's college professors when Yale inquired concerning the young man's character and scholarship: "He wants action of an heroic sort—though not mock-heroic." And Dean Weigle added this comment: "The fact that those words were written eleven years ago [eleven years before the *Dorchester* incident] in answer to our inquiry about him while he was still a senior in college gives them all the more value now."

When he came to his high hour, he found more than "one other man"; he found many men, and the other *"One"* was there.

The prayer he asked me to pray when we talked in Philadelphia, the only prayer he wanted, was answered.

He was adequate.

And who would not want that prayer answered? Who would not be adequate?

Well, you may be! Farmer, merchant, miner, doctor,

33

preacher, public official, teacher, pupil in the school, mother in the home, athlete, or whatever—*you* may be adequate. Here is the right prayer, the prayer that never fails of the answer: "Ask and it shall be given you."

Now that prayer is presently to have a shrine. We have given the summit of Wolf Hill, where he so often went and where he found something of the significance of the ancient Mount of Sacrifice, a new name, his name. Already it is a shrine, an interfaith shrine, but eventually there will be a memorial there, simple but worthy to each of the four chaplains, with an eternal light shining down into the valley of the Contoocook. In the peace, it will tell men that beyond all else there is a unity that transcends their differences of faith and race and color.

That shrine and light tell me something more—they tell me that the prayer of faith is *always* answered and that it is the road to Peace with Power.

V

An Inheritance

PRAYER to those who possess and use it is first an inheritance. It is difficult to believe that there is any person who does not pray or has not prayed, though there are some who dismiss prayer altogether. Foreign Minister Vishinsky of Russia said to United States Senator Alexander Wiley of Wisconsin: "I do not pray." But prayer is of many forms, and may be to any one of many gods. Prayer is adulation and communion, praise and grateful obeisance, as well as petition and supplication. The Greeks and Romans and those who preceded them had unnumbered gods and nearly as many altars. Today Communism is a dynamic, passionate religion and Russia has at least two gods: Lenin and Stalin. Mr. Vishinsky meant that he did not pray to Senator Wiley's god.

But we do not enter here. The only prayer we know as the road to Peace with Power is the prayer that claims the promise of Jesus Christ: "Whatsoever ye shall ask

35

in my name, that will I do" and "If ye shall ask anything *in my name, I will do it."*

The prayer never fails. That promise stands fast. And that prayer is first of all our inheritance. I received it from my parents as they received it from theirs. With my face buried in the calico that covered my mother's knees and with her worn, gentle hands on my head, I uttered the first prayers of childhood. The faith my father declared from the pulpit he nailed together became my faith.

The prayers of my parents and their faith have companioned me through the years. Memory becomes more vivid as time passes. The low and armless rocker behind the airtight wood stove in the Oregon sitting room where my mother comforted her children was an altar too. Always in the morning an open Bible lay upon it. There she had worshipped before other members of the family were astir. There she found the strength for her crowded day, and there she breathed deeply of the grace she breathed upon us all.

Once when I lay with a broken body in a Massachusetts hospital, her prayer came to me, claiming life and recovery for me. "I have the answer," she wired. "Psalm 91:15-16." And presently I read: "He shall call upon me and I will answer him, I will be with him in trouble: I will deliver him and honor him. With long life will I satisfy him and show him my salvation."

It was a command to recover. She had the answer. She knew and I believed. Crushed hips, fractured vertebrae and ribs, internal injuries—nothing for science to do but wait, and for ten days without hope, but she "had the answer."

The last time I saw her she came out of a coma to greet her reunited family. For the first time in years the six children and their father were all together and with her. I had flown across the continent to join the reunion, and on the late evening of the day when I must return I was alone with her.

As I knelt by her bed she said, "Put your face upon my hands for I cannot lift them to your head." And then as her lips brushed my hair she whispered, "My son, if when you come again I am not here to greet you as always I have greeted you before, then, my son, you will know where to find me!" And with that sure knowledge I left her and flew into the East.

Prayer, the road to Peace with Power, is my inheritance.

And had my parents not taught me, had there been in them nothing to give, society and the community would have bestowed upon me the religious heritage from the believing past—schools, hospitals, churches, and all the traditions of faith and practice. Only those who have lived where the Bible has not gone and where Judaeo-Christianity has not penetrated have completely escaped this inheritance.

But increasingly prayer to me is something more than an inheritance; it is *infinitely* more than an inheritance; it is my experience, my day-by-day experience. And as an experience, prayer must become an achievement if it is to be for all the vicissitudes and for every circumstance of life, the road to Peace with Power.

In the first paragraph of this book I wrote that I had a sense of mission: "to share with others a reality that through all the varying fortunes of life has never failed." In these pages I am opening my heart, baring my soul, putting down the most sacred things because I know that for all who have burdens too great for them to bear alone, prayer can be your answer as it has been and is mine, because I know that you too may have Peace with Power.

This book is a story—or rather many stories—and the purpose is not to convince, though the purpose will fail if conviction does not follow. But the single purpose is to share with others an experience made up of many experiences that gathers momentum through the years. To share, and in sharing to hope and indeed pray that the story itself will persuade those who read to test the formula and make it their own: "Ask and it shall be given you."

VI

Prayer Is Always Answered

I HAVE WRITTEN several times already that prayer, prayer as I have experienced it, is always answered and that always prayer is the way to Peace with Power. I have written too that my story is, or may become, a formula for you, that you may have Peace with Power. *Then how?*

The answer to that question, the very heart of it, is in the great promise of "Ask and it shall be given you— for anyone that asketh receiveth (Old Testament Apocrypha). It has been variously phrased by Jesus: "Whatsoever ye shall ask in my name, that will I do" and "If ye shall ask anything in my name, I will do it" and "Ask what ye will and it shall be done unto you" and many others.

Always the emphasis is upon and the promise of the answer conditioned upon "Ask." Simple enough? Yes, but imperative too.

There is another great and timely message from God

to man: "Behold, I have set before you an open door and no man can shut it." Now what is a door for? A door is an entrance. Those who wish to come into what lies beyond cross the threshold, use the door. For those who do not use the door, it might as well be closed. The open door is an invitation.

Prayer is God's open door to comfort, forgiveness, reassurance, courage, and to Peace with Power. He invites and repeats the invitation again and again—"Ask!" The invitation becomes a veritable challenge, and everywhere and speaking from all the generations of the past and present are the voices of those who confirm the good faith of the invitation, who say: "I did ask and I received."

But you may reply in good faith: "I would be inexpressibly happy to believe as you believe. I have all the human needs that could be described. Yes, burdens, many burdens too great for me to bear alone. And I have prayed or tried to pray, but my prayers are words and only words—nothing happens. My faith is just too small and it seems there is nothing I can do about it. I only doubt when I would believe."

But there is something you *can* do about it. Something definite, reasonable, and immediate.

First: Doubt your doubts. Make this the basic philosophy of your life when you regard the constructive relationships of your life and also when you turn to prayer and to God. There is downright intellectual honesty in this attitude.

You have friends. Are you ever tempted to doubt them? Well, doubt that doubt—first. Not your friends, but your doubt of their friendship. Many—too many—

people are forever unhappy themselves and making those who love them unhappy because of a miserable, negative attitude toward those who love them and whom they deeply love.

I remember an occasion after World War I when in a Washington D.C. hotel lobby a typical male scandal-monger was regaling a group of men he had called into a close huddle with an evil story involving the President of the United States. As he finished, the fellow said, "And what do you think of that?" A young man still in uniform had the answer for him, "What do I think of that? Why, sir, I think that is a lie and you, sir, are a liar." Right there the man proved himself a coward as well as a liar.

Call your doubt a liar when it would hurt the good, injure some fine relationship of life, set you against your friends, your faith, your better self.

Certainly you must face facts, but be sure they are facts, not merely rumors. Do not be blind to reality, but be sure you are not deceived by some counterfeit.

Doubt your doubts before you doubt your beliefs.

Reverse the order.

Doubt your doubts first.

Years ago I formed the habit of saying the first thing in the morning, *"I believe."* It has become a fixed habit. I may be in a Pullman berth or flying high above some ocean, but I greet the dawn with "I believe"—those two words.

When I stand to say them, as I prefer, and when I speak them out clearly, as I prefer (though on occasion they may be unspoken), I find in them physical exercise as well as moral. I cannot say them without lifting my shoulders a little and standing more erect. . . . "I believe," and the day for me is well begun.

With equal honesty I could say, "I doubt" or "I deny," and there are many things a man must doubt and deny just to be decent. But *"I believe"* is affirmative, positive; and when you say it and mean it, you are on the march.

I believe in my country and in the American Dream. In democracy, as within the genius of what we call the American way of life, democracy has been realized and is being more and more perfected.

I believe in my fellow men in spite of all that I know about some of them and may have suffered from them.

I believe in myself—in spite of what I too well know about myself. I believe in myself, not as I have been or am, but as, God helping me, I purpose to become.

And I believe in God. Right here again I would enter upon the record my own experiences. At the first I believed in God all right, but my belief was a misunderstanding, a fear and even a hate until I saw and found God in and through Jesus Christ. Until I thus saw and found God, consciously at first and as I grew older unconsciously and I suppose subconsciously, I associated Him with a picture in the family Bible—a bearded, angry man with a sword high above his head, driving two little people (Adam and Eve) before Him. To me God was then a particular and a fearful person. But Jesus came to me and Jesus forgave. "Neither do I condemn thee, go sin no more," He said, and now God was speaking. Jesus gathered the mistaken, hungry people about him and fed them—He never drove them out of any garden or from any good. Jesus took little children into His arms and re-

42

buked the rugged men who tried to push them aside:
"Suffer them to come unto me," He said, "and forbid
them not, for of such is the Kingdom of Heaven." Jesus
crossed every social frontier and broke through the cries
of "unclean, unclean" to heal the lepers. When I heard
Jesus say to me, "Come and see," and accepted that invitation, I said, "Now I know what God is like. He is like
that!"

Presently a great light broke over me and I knew that
Jesus had made God real to me, that in Jesus God had
come alive to me. To me Jesus had become completely
God.

In this manner I believe in and experienced God.

First then, doubt your doubts if you would find in
prayer your road to Peace with Power.

Second: Begin where you are and with the faith you
have—or begin even without faith. Yes, just that.

It does not take a great faith to get a great answer.

It is the faith you use, or the faith you would like to
have and cry out for, that moves the mountain.

A man came to Jesus with his little son who was mentally ill. All other journeys had led only to disappoint-
ment; all other promised cures had failed. Jesus looked at
the man and at the child and heard the story. Then He
asked a question, and what a question! *"Do you believe?"*
Imagine that! After everything he had suffered, after all
he had experienced of disillusionment and defeat, to be
asked that question. I could understand any sharp and
even angry reply that father might have made to the
question of this unknown, this condemned, this always
variously regarded "healer." But the man met the mood

of Jesus, met it with sheer honesty the like of which the world has not often heard. He said:

"I believe, help thou mine unbelief."

Just that and nothing more. So little faith and even that mixed with greater doubt. But it was enough, indeed it was an abundance—it cured the boy.

You see, that father said "I believe" first. He believed his belief first and doubted his doubt last, and what was first in his mind and heart won over the doubt and destroyed the power of unbelief.

Jesus said: "If ye have faith as a grain of mustard seed . . . nothing shall be impossible unto you."

A mustard seed is just about the smallest of all the seeds that live and germinate. Faith so small as that is enough to move your "mountain" if you will use it.

A good many years ago I met a man who had always lived a robust and frequently an evil life. He became profoundly concerned for his present and future. He said, "I believe, help my unbelief." I remember then his first prayer. He had insisted that he could not pray, but at last he prayed audibly just two words: "O God." He had used those words often before, but never before to such a purpose. Now they were quite enough to bring him Peace with Power.

If you want Peace with Power, "Ask and it shall be given you."

The prayer God answers first is the prayer: "I believe, help thou mine unbelief."

The prayer God answers first is the sincere and even inarticulate cry for *Faith*.

44

Do You Want the Answer?

My FIRST ANSWERED PRAYER was as easy as falling out of bed and claiming an ancient promise for a present need. My second answered prayer kept me on my knees or walking a long night through—a night of bitter anguish and, before I had the answer, a night of frustration and disillusionment. There have been other nights almost like that night when I demanded of God the recovery of my brother, though more frequently it has been as direct and simple as "Ask and it shall be given you."

Prayer in all the particulars is as personal as it is universal, and it measures its ministry to the limitations as well as to the needs of those who pray.

On my first visit to Palestine a young Arab clergyman of the Anglican Church guided me to the brook Jabok which flows into the Jordan from the east and some distance below the Lake of Galilee. Here occurred the greatest wrestling match in human history; here Jacob matched himself against the angel and though the angel broke his thigh, Jacob stayed through to win the decision.

My friend took me to a spot back from the traditional sight. There a great crack appears in the sandstone. Pointing to the opening, he said, "It is a tradition of my people that Jacob was losing to the angel when he thrust his foot deep into that crack and locked it there; and though the angel could twist and break him, Jacob could not be dislodged." . . . "I will not let thee go until thou bless me," Jacob cried, and his cry prevailed.

He carried the limp until he died, but he had his answer.

There are times when faith must be as stubborn as that. If the stakes are high enough, if the reason justifies the all-night vigil, then pray without ceasing, "battering the gates of Heaven with storms of prayer," as Tennyson put it. . . . *Always you may have the answer.*

One of man's most imperative prayers is the prayer against fear. That the prayer itself is not limited to any orthodox conception of it is suggested by the fact that Gene Tunney, former undefeated heavyweight champion of the world, has written a profoundly moving story of his prayer to overcome a fear that threatened to defeat him even before he entered the ring. His whole body was mastered by the fear and his mind was possessed by it. Only his heart could cry out for "the Living God."

Well, that cry was heard, and it was enough—Gene Tunney rose from a bed that had all but collapsed under his trembling, got up to be completely master of himself and, incidentally, to master his opponent.

One morning in the spring of 1918 I was assisting

bearers from an advanced first-aid dressing station near Menil-le-Tours. Four men to a stretcher, we were carrying out the body of a captain who had been killed the night before and a wounded German prisoner whose legs were so terribly mangled that he died later as he was being lifted into an ambulance.

At one point it was necessary for us to leave the protection of the trench which had caved in under concentrated shell fire. We lifted the stretchers to the parapet and started down across an open field toward battalion headquarters. The morning was damp and filled with mist. We wore armbands and carried Red Cross flags, and though the lines at that point were hardly a hundred yards apart, it is doubtful whether the enemy could distinguish more than a small concentration of men in the field. A barrage of three-inch high explosive shells was put down on the field. The experience will never be forgotten by those who lived through it. We ran first with the stretchers and then without them. Then remembering instructions—it was the first experience of the kind for some of us—we flung ourselves face down in the oozing mud. A lad just in front of me was lifted by the shell that blew up deep under him. That all of us were not killed was due to the fact that penetration in the soft earth was so deep.

When we were well under cover again, with shame we remembered the stretchers left behind us in the field. To be sure, only one man had been alive when we left the advanced station and he was an enemy, but that made no difference. We had failed.

Then we went back. Again the enemy opened fire.

47

Again the earth rose in geysers all about us. That was my second bout with stark terror. I had argued with myself that it wasn't my party anyhow, that I wasn't under orders, that I had just volunteered to help. But it was no good. I knew myself for what I was—a coward. Then I prayed! My prayer was an unvoiced shouting agony in my soul. I remember now that it was like this: "God help me not to run again!" And He did help me. I went out and came back and went out again. Until night fell and the danger was past, God kept His promise; and in keeping that promise with me gave other men, perhaps as frightened as I, fortitude to stay it through.

There is a courage perhaps greater than the courage of the four chaplains (though such comparisons are always invidious). I have a young friend just entering his career, a career that becomes increasingly a ministry of unselfish service to others. Now suddenly a malignancy stops him dead in his tracks and takes away part of his face. Did I say "stops him"? Then I have miswritten. Straight ahead he goes. With confidence that marvels us, he claims the promise "Ask and it shall be given you." He puts that promise squarely in God's will for him, justifies our faith to claim with him the promise, and demonstrates every day Peace with Power.

It is the strength and courage to "stay through" that on occasion you and I and every other man and woman find to be the immediate and imperative requirement. No task however humble and no situation however remote from the spectacular are beyond "His love and care" if it is a task or a situation for which you and I are responsible. The one thing required and all that is required is that we shall "ask." It is written that He is more willing and eager to bestow than we are to ask. Unbelievable perhaps, but as of my experience true.

Be reasonably sure that you want *the* answer, *His* answer to your prayer, before you pray. For your prayer may be a disillusioning or even dangerous thing, as on occasion prayer has become for me. But why pray at all if yours is the only answer you will accept? Surely I may have my strong desire, my passionate purpose. Surely the invitation to "ask" does not shut out the expressing of what my mind holds and my heart contains. But in such a case "in His name" is the key to the great door. "Not my will but Thine be done" at last makes the prayer right and perfect. And with that goes the assurance that in all the years since that night when His "No" became my "Yes," he has never failed me—the assurance that I need never turn away from any prayer without at least the clear knowledge that *I have been heard.*

The final answer may be delayed—and delay is indeed hard to bear—but delay itself is an answer. I have found that answer satisfying too.

Particularly difficult are those situations in which there are alternatives. Emerson has said that there can never be two duties confronting a person, that always one of the apparent two, and only one, is duty. Very well, but so often the second looks so imperative and immediate that only the wisdom of Solomon, which I do not have, is competent to make a sure, right choice.

Once I was invited to become president of a college on

the Pacific coast. The offer was most attractive and the opportunity very great. But already I had a position and opportunity equally attractive. I spent weeks thinking, studying, weighing—and praying. I got nowhere. The entire family became absorbed with my search for the right answer. Indeed it was a family search, as it so often is in these grave matters. Finally a decision had to be reached within the week, and in my own mind I was no nearer that decision than when I began the search.

One night with Mrs. Poling I sat down and made a ledger account. On one side I listed all the reasons and arguments for going and on the other all those for staying. In cold, dry ink, "Go" had it. Then I prayed again, this time as I would talk with another friend. I said, "It looks like California. But I am still uncertain. Fence that road for me if I should not go. Stop me!" I had the sure feeling that my prayer was fair, that it was the right prayer. I had not dodged the issue and I had done all I knew to reach a decision. Again I wanted to put my life where it would count for the most. Either decision seemed conducive to this, and I needed guidance from without and beyond my own wisdom and that of my family and friends.

That prayer was answered. A dangerous prayer it was, and I knew it. The road was fenced, not only fenced but *blocked*. Presently I could not have gone.

Again and again I have offered that same prayer. In the most intimate experiences and choices of my life that prayer has opened the way for me—or closed it. Made the meaning clear and the purpose plain.

Such a prayer could become an alibi or an excuse, an easy shifting of responsibility; but always you will know, and of course God knows.

He does not fence your road or keep it open when you can build your own barrier or take it down.

VIII

What God Does Not Promise

G<small>OD</small> never promises exemption. He does promise companionship, which is better. He does not promise to deliver you or me or any other individual from pain, sorrow, economic disaster, or "what have you." But He does give the assurance that He will help us through and that there will be compensations. "I will not leave you comfortless, I will come to you." These are the words of Jesus.

And this more needs saying: nowhere in either the Old Testament or the New are we assured special well-being because of piety. Indeed there are instances as in the great drama of Job when goodness itself is tested and make a vehicle of trial. Even Paul cried to be relieved of his "thorn in the flesh," but cried in vain; and his contemporaries, the disciples, including Peter and the faithful who were hunted through the Roman catacombs and burned along the Appian Way and fed to the lions in the

Colosseum, were not relieved of their physical ordeals because they were holy. But that never-disregarded promise "I will come to you" was kept with each of them and it is written that they chose—it was their choice—"to suffer affliction" as the faithful had suffered in earlier time rather than to "enjoy" what Rome at her voluptuous best had to offer. It is even more baldly stated, if you please: "For whom the Lord loveth He chasteneth and scourgeth every son whom he receiveth." Surely these are words hard to understand. Indeed they are not to be understood this side of that "time enough" of which the great Horace Bushnell spoke—that unhurried eternal moment when the hidden things shall be revealed and when we shall find the answers for the questions remaining unanswered and for the problems yet unsolved.

The appalling suffering of the best eminent and good and the problem of human suffering itself remain as the great unsolvables of time, nor do I ever blink that issue. But this I do know. God comes to these and grants them mercies and foregleams of that which is theirs presently to possess. I have seen them in veritable ecstasies upon their death beds. We might reasonably curse and die as Job's friends recommended to him, if this life were all. Those who believe it to be all and who so insist are to be understood when they curse. But this life is definitely not all! That too is for the one who writes these sentences an experience.

I believe in eternal life because it has been a personal experience for me ever more increasing since a certain February morning in 1918. With an orderly I waited in the rain at the head of a communicating trench north of

Toul in France. A platoon from a United States machine-gun company was coming out. The first lieutenant
who brought up the rear stopped to inquire the way to
the nearest canteen. He was sick and fever burned in his
tired face. "Tonsillitis," he said as he leaned on his stick,
"and trenchfoot." Then pulling himself together, he
stumbled on after his men. When he had gone a very
short distance, a three-inch shell "let go" in the middle
of his platoon. Hearing it coming, we flung ourselves flat
in the mud, and then at the screams of agony we hurried
over to the wounded and dead. We looked after those
who still needed the little we could do for them and gathered up the fragments of the others.

There on the bloody highway of France I experienced
immortality. I knew that the lieutenant with the aching
throat, the lad whose sick eyes had looked into mine, the
boy with whom I had just talked was not in what I had
just picked up. I had not talked to *that*. But also I knew
he was somewhere. I knew that there had been authority
enough to begin his life, to carry it from his mother's
womb to the awful end on a shell-scarred road of France.
Short of immortality I had the choice of just two con-
clusions: 1) either creative authority willed to leave that
personality there in the blood and muck, willed to end it
in such a sorry fashion; or 2) the same authority which
could create was unable to continue, was helpless before
the event, was without resources beyond that road in front
of Toul.

Either conclusion was to me unreasonable. Both my
heart and mind rejected them. That young man stopped
where I picked up his battered body, or he went on. I

knew then, as I know now, that he went on. It was not a debate then and is not now. It was not an argument. It was an experience so real that it left me at the moment all but disinterested in the body. And as I write now, that experience is even more vivid than it was on that February morning more than thirty years ago.

I know that those whose forms I touch when only their forms remain, when to my touch there is no responsive pressure, have by the divine miracle survived. Also I know where to find them. And there is something more—yes, definitely. That in you which is destined to live forever is alive now and shall never die.

That experience of immortality is closely related to another experience, the experience of Jesus Christ as "very God of very God." "Because I live, ye shall live also," He said, and "Whosoever liveth and believeth in me shall never die." Since this is so, since there is the greater and better part beyond what for want of a better name we call death, why should I ever give the dignity of finality to this little portion of life, or grieve over much because of suffering or disaster about which that great realist the Apostle Paul had this to say: "Our light affliction, which is but for a moment, worketh for us a far more exceeding and eternal weight of glory." There is now and also eternally a ministry in pain and compensation for suffering.

My own more intimate understanding of this great fact and my personal acceptance of the ministry of pain came with an accident about which I shall write more fully in a later chapter. I know now that I would never have chosen that all-but-fatal ordeal, particularly with its near death for members of my family. Even now the memory of its particulars and of the tortured nights before I began to recover is sometimes a nightmare.

But I also know that I could not have taken from me what has come to me out of that experience without suffering intellectual, moral, and family losses that would be infinite. I would not choose again what took me so near death, but it does not seem that I could live without what that experience added to my life. Here you too may find, if you have not already found it—or perhaps as yet you have not known a circumstance that laid the test—here you too may find Peace with Power.

Very Personal

Twice under unusual and very poignant circumstances, once in a general hospital in England in 1943 and again in France more than a year later, I talked with wounded men about immortality. What I write now is a composite of the two experiences, though it centers in France. Also my niece Kathleen Phelps, a remarkable girl who was a senior nurse in the most advanced station on the Ledo Road, is always in my thoughts as I write. Her fiancé was shot down over Sicily and soon after, before she knew that he would not return, she contracted cerebral malaria in the jungle. She survived this practically 100 per cent fatal disease and with indomitable courage lived long enough to return to her people where, until she died, she was like a torch to light their way ahead.

It was in a general hospital in France that I sat by the bed of a boy from Georgia. The chaplain had said, "He wants to talk to you. He remembers when you spoke in his home town. He was just a kid then and went to hear you with his father, and he's been waiting for you ever since he heard you were coming." The medical major nodded assent and added, "It's all right; he's dying, and knows it. It won't hurt him to talk."

The boy's shaven head was bandaged. There had been a head wound, as well as others, and deep burns when his tank was blown up under him. His eyes, that seldom left mine in the next half-hour, were dark and sunken. His lips were cracked and fevered. Now and then the nurse came and moistened them with cotton dipped in a solution. He always smiled and turned his head to thank her. Thoughtfully the girl drew the curtains, and we were alone.

"Sir," the boy began, "I'm not afraid to die. I have settled that. But one thing keeps coming up to bother me —all that I'm going to leave behind. I've had a lot of time to think about that, and I can't get away from it. I guess you'd call it feeling sorry for myself?" He smiled —smiled so infectiously that I smiled back at him.

"Sir, did you ever feel that you just couldn't get over losing some things—even for Heaven?" And the boy smiled again, only now there was an infinite hunger in the strong face.

"Yes," I said, "I know the feeling. I knew it first when they spoiled the old swimming hole. They put in locks on the Yamhill River in Oregon and sank the 'lower landing' under six feet of water. I just couldn't get over it, John. The channel where we dived for mussels and the sandbank where we lay in the sun and talked were gone forever."

The boy from Georgia smiled softly and turned his head with understanding. "You make me think of my catfish lines in the river," he said, and seemed eagerly waiting for me to go on.

"Well," I continued, "I was in the East when it happened, and a few years later when I went back I thought at first that I couldn't look at the place, but my curiosity took me right there. And then everything was different. I had the old swimming hole, John—had it forever."

The boy on the bed was breathing faster, and his eyes were intense.

"It was like this," I went on. "The channel where we dived for the mussels and the sand where we lay in the sun were not under the water. They were in me! I hadn't left them behind; I had brought them along! They—and a thousand other memories of beautiful things—are all with me. I can never go back to them, but I have brought them all along."

The boy from Georgia waited and then said, "But—" And I knew what he would have said.

"I've thought of that too," I continued. "I used to fear death, not because of what I knew about it, but because of what I didn't know. It was fear of the unknown, and that fear is the only final, baffling fear, John."

He nodded his assent. I wondered then whether I could put into words what has become very real to me, so real that it is an experience as comforting as the grip of a friend's hand. I'd never tried to say it before, but the boy from Georgia was waiting—and I had gone too far to turn back.

"In 1935 I was in Singapore," I said, "when I received

61

word that my father was seriously ill. The twelve thousand miles that separated us was the most appalling reality that I had ever known. To be twelve thousand miles away and helpless! But a few years later, when my mother died, I suddenly discovered that there were now no separating distances and no dividing oceans. After she died, and ever since, we have been together. And now it is like that with my son. As I think of those whose physical presence I shall never know again, always I think of them as with me, and there is no interference, no interruption, and no end of knowing."

John was listening, though his eyes were far away; then he said something that I shall never forget. He said, "I've had that same feeling about Ray—my buddy—who was killed by an anti-personnel mine on Utah Beach the day I was first hit. He died without saying a word. Just before it got him, he yelled to me, 'Down! Machine-gun nest!'— thinking of me, sir. I crawled to him, but there was nothing I could do."

The boy was speaking with increasing difficulty, but I knew he had something to say that couldn't wait, and I didn't interrupt. He went on, as though fascinated by his own words. "His head wasn't hurt. I put my face against his, and then I knew that Ray wasn't there. But I knew something more, sir; I knew that he was somewhere! His body was smashed, but he wasn't. I can't tell you why I knew it, but nothing else made sense. Every day now, that feeling is stronger. Ray isn't dead. He's around! Tell me —" and his voice rose—"Am I kidding myself? Am I crazy?"

I shook my head. "No, you're not kidding yourself."

As John talked, I had been thinking of a road in front of Toul in France and of my World War I experience already related in this book. That February morning I had learned what the boy from Georgia was talking about now.

"No," I said, "you're not kidding yourself, and you're not crazy. Ray wasn't there, and he was somewhere—he is somewhere. John, either the Power that began Ray's life and carried him from under his mother's heart to Utah Beach was willing to see him end like that, or the Power that could create could not continue, was helpless before that mine—it had no other resources. John, either of those alternatives just doesn't make sense."

Then I went a little deeper, for the boy from Georgia was still waiting and understanding, I think, better than I understood. "You learned before you went to college, John, that nothing in nature is ever annihilated. Forms change and patterns of life, but life itself goes on. I do not try to anticipate the details, but I do know that a mine couldn't stop Ray. To think that a law which operates everywhere else ceases to operate in life's highest expression—in personality, in Ray—just doesn't make sense."

The boy from Georgia strained to lift his head from the pillow. "Then you believe," he whispered, as though half afraid to give his thought a voice, "you do believe," he repeated, "that they wait for us and that we shall know them?"

"Yes," I replied, "I believe that, because I believe that it is after what we call death, John, that life—your life and mine and Ray's—really begins. I believe that this life is but our childhood. And, of course, if you and I live beyond the grave, if you and I do go on, then that which makes it possible for us to know each other now—the 'you' of you—goes on, too, and just as we remember here, we shall recognize each other there. I can't prove it, John, but I believe it—I am very sure about it. Yes, and my belief has become my experience. John, it is as real to me as the bed in which you lie!"

He turned his head a little, as though listening to another voice than mine, and whispered, "I believe it too, and it makes God very frendly—just like your own father."

I felt that I had stayed long enough, but when he recognized my purpose to leave, an eagerness came into both his face and voice. "No, please don't go yet. Tell me something more."

And I told him then the inner thoughts of a man who has found his answer to the great fear. "John, all the beauty I have ever known, and all my friendships, all that I have well remembered, I have brought along. Only 'things' are left behind. I am sure, so sure that I no longer question, that while I do not know the country to which I travel, I shall have friends waiting for me there, who do know it."

I remembered then strange lands to which I had traveled, but lands that were not strange when I came to them because I was not a stranger to those who came to meet me. There was an almost supernatural intensity in the boy's gaze as with his eyes he held me, held me as though he would keep me to my course, and so I went on and told him as I have written it in this book, the story of my mother:

"A month before my mother died, I flew out to Oregon to spend a few days with her in the old home. She had been an invalid for several years, but her mind was alert, and when I left her she said, "My son, if when you come again I am not here to greet you as always I have greeted you before—then, my son, you will know where to find me!"

Now I knew that I had finished my visit. The face of the boy from Georgia was more beautiful than any sunset. He pushed his burned right hand, which was bandaged as big as a toy balloon, across the sheet, and I reached out my hand and steadied it. Then he said, "Sir, please pray."

I do not remember my words in the prayer, only these words that are not mine: "Let not your heart be troubled: ye believe in God; believe also in Me. . . . I go to prepare a place for you."

The boy did not open his eyes as I stood up to go, but he said, "I'm taking them all along, sir, and I'll be seeing you!"

As I went away, it seemed to me that the ward and the entire hospital were filled with Peace and Power.

X

The Prayer of Gratitude

Prayer has many parts, but prayer is one. It is a unity—human and divine. Man and God are in conversation and man makes a mistake when he monopolizes the conversation. Prayer is even more a listening than a talking.

Once Raymond Robins, Alaskan adventurer, lawyer, and orator, friend and adviser of Presidents, co-worker with Jane Addams, reformer, evangelist, and Christian statesman, one of the most eminent men among all men I have known, came to Long House, our New Hampshire home. That evening is unforgettable. The boys, stretched in front of the fire and scarcely breathing at times, gave rapt attention as Robins talked. That night as never before in our long friendship, I heard him talk. He seemed inspired. Afterward he said, "It was the silence, the concentrated silence of those boys that kept me going after I got started."

For me, prayer in its simplest forms as well as in its

supreme experiences has been a "listening." I am sure
that I have missed much—too much—because I have not
listened oftener and harder.

Once traveling by rail from Louisville to Cincinnati,
after reading in the New Testament, I stopped, dropped
my chin into my cupped hand, closed my eyes, and with my
face pressed against the window, waited. I became completely alone and quiet in that crowded coach. I was entirely unconscious of the man seated beside me. The assurance that possessed me, the calm and peace that
enveloped me were as nothing I had ever known before.
I saw no face, I had no vision, but the Presence rode with
me and spoke to me until the conductor called my station,
and then he called twice.

That morning on the train is a red-letter memory.
There have been other times of the same quality and just
as real, but never another more intense. From that "conversation" where I said not a word, and to which I made
no other contribution than my attitude of listening, came
resources of strength for unknown ordeals ahead, experiences that could not be anticipated—resources of
strength that to this hour I have drawn upon.

Prayer is listening. Prayer is communion. Prayer is
conversation with a friend who is all-wise and all-
competent, a friend who always has something important
to say if he can get my ear.

There is one invitation that God never fails to accept.
The invitation voiced by the boy Samuel, whose mother
brought him to the High Priest Eli and gave him to God
as she had promised: "Speak, Lord, for Thy servant

68

heareth." And that is all you need to say or think if you would hear the *Voice*—if then you will listen.

One book among all the volumes in the prayer library I have read has been an inspiring guide in my prayer life —Harry Emerson Fosdick's *The Meaning of Prayer*. I read it first when it was in its first edition. Often I have read it since and always I keep it near at hand. Scholarly, personal, and at grips with the every-day issues of life, it is timeless. For you and for me today it is as vital and practical too as it was more than thirty years ago when I first opened it. I refer to no other volume here because I would avoid confusion. The Bible and *The Meaning of Prayer* are enough, though many other books have a message for you as they have had a message for me.

The prayer of gratitude is one of the most dynamic of all prayers. It may be a simple thank-you, and as brief as that, and of course it may be longer. Sometimes it is a volume—as in this book, for through these pages, line after line, sentence following sentence, I have sought to say my thank-you to God who has heard and understood, who always has answered, and who has never failed. I have failed others, I have failed myself, I have failed Him— He never has! But the prayer of gratitude, perhaps the most rewarding of all prayers, is the one we forget. I am, and perhaps you are, very much like the small boy of a story. Given an apple by "the kind lady," he at once went vigorously to work. Mortified and embarrassed, the lad's mother said, "Why, son, haven't you anything to say?" and son said it. Without missing a beat he said, "Have you got any more?"

Much of man's praying is like that. We take and we take for granted and then with our mouths full, with our lives overflowing with goodness and with the future in His care, forgetting to say thank you, we shout for "more."

Another has said that "a single grateful thought toward Heaven is the most perfect prayer."

But there is something that needs saying concerning gratitude when we, because of a real or fancied service we may have rendered, look for it in others. "He who receives a good turn should never forget it; he who does one should never remember it" is the sound advice of the ancient. My father, whom I followed into the ministry, made that advice realistic when he told me that I should never do anything with the expectation that I would be thanked for it or be gratefully regarded. "Do it because you must, or should, or are happy to—and forget it! Then if someone is grateful and reminds you, fine! If not, as will be more often the case, nothing rankles; you're not unhappy." I have found it to be sound advice that I have at least tried to follow.

Gratitude does something to the one who receives it and enriches life generally, though there are times when, as Henry Ward Beecher remarked, "next to ingratitude, the most painful thing to hear is gratitude." But chiefly and always gratitude enriches the life of the one who is grateful and who finds a way to express it.

Happiness and gratitude are twins and one cannot live apart from the other. They are qualities of the mind and soul and not things in the hand. The poor fellow who is forever trying to be happy is doomed to failure from the beginning. Trying to be happy is like trying to fall asleep, or trying to fall in love. Happiness is a by-product. One has said that happiness is a shy nymph, found more often at the door of the poor than at the gate of the rich, and that when you chase her, always you lose her, but that when you go on about your business of living and loving and serving, she comes and abides. Gratitude is like that. You cannot force yourself to be grateful, but only the grateful heart ever knows Peace with Power.

The most expressive story of this union of gratitude and happiness was written by Irving Bacheller, who told of his search for the happiest person in the world and of how, to find that person, he traveled the world over and around. He sat with the wise and great. He talked with men and women young and old, rich and poor, but returned unsuccessful from his quest.

Then he went for a vacation and rest into the mountains of the South. For two weeks he lived in the cabin home of a widowed mountain mother—and right there he found his happiest person. Her hands were callused and she was bent under her years and hardships, but there was no doubt about it, she was that happiest person.

As he was leaving the mountains, he said, in effect, as I now recall the story, "You are the happiest person I have ever known, but, Mother, how can you be happy? Happy in your poverty, happy in your childbearing and child rearing, happy now in your straitened circumstances and loneliness?" And the mountain woman answered, "But, sir, how can I help it? With my children to love and to work for and with the love of God in my heart!"

There is the answer—love and work and God, and who

shall say that the mountain woman, who had gratitude and happiness, did not have Peace with Power?

There is one prayer that should not be offered—the prayer that deliberately seeks to buy Heaven's favor and God's gifts. Granted that the ancient scriptures are filled with such prayers, they are foreign to the mind of Christ and to His Spirit, for He gave His blessings without regard. God cannot be bought off, or on. Even as "the quality of mercy is not strained," and blesses him that gives and him that receives, the just and unjust alike, so God's gifts are not conditioned upon our knowledge of them, nor upon our ability to repay them.

But when in gratitude for God's gifts, and in the spirit of the mountain woman, we share our relative much with those who have little; when we build institutions of healing and cultural enrichment; when we establish foundations to serve mankind's common need; or hand even our crust of bread to the hungry; or a cup of cold water to the thirsty; we are saying a worthy and acceptable thank-you to God, the Father of us all.

Then it is that you and I, even as the mother in the mountain cabin, with hearts of gratitude first, and then with deeds that express it, find happiness on the road that leads to Peace with Power.

XI

United Prayer

My FIRST PRAYER to an answer was not entirely my own achievement. It was a composite prayer, a united prayer. Many prayers flowed into mine, and the very appointments of the room arranged by other hands than mine contributed to the "answer."

I was in my father's house and a student in the struggling, pioneer college he and others of his courage and faith had founded. The motto, silver letters on a green card that called me out of my despair and inspired me to action, had been hung on the wall of that room for the eyes of her children to see, by the hands of my mother; and when I told her of my prayer, there was no doubt in the words of her encouragement. She knelt then beside my bed and prayed with me. Soon my father was with us too.

The professor of Public Speech in that college came to talk with me. As his kindly eyes looked down upon me that day and as he listened to my story, he nodded, brushed back his hair with a characteristic gesture, and said, "You'll do it all right, Dan, you'll do it," and before he left that room David Metzger prayed with me. . . . A few years ago he came to Saranac Lake and presently died with the dread disease that steadily yields to science, but still remains unconquered. Do you question why recovery was denied him? Well, he had no questions, and when the summons came to him so far from the scenes he loved, he had the answer, too, and was waiting. Of this important matter we shall write in a later chapter.

And there were other faculty members who came to my room to give me added assurance, and not a voice was raised to question my answer. "That was a simple, child-like faith," you say. Yes, it was a simple faith, but those who held it with me were not simpletons nor were they childish. They were rugged and on occasion heavy-handed too. They were close to the covered-wagon period (some of the wagons themselves were still thereabouts). They were of the pioneer tradition and close to those who had laid the foundations of home, school, church, and state along that little river. One professor who stood by that day before I went to speak was an Amherst-Yale man who not only read and taught Greek but spoke it rather fluently. But when he prayed with me, his language was simple and childlike.

My teammates came. We had a championship basket-ball team that year with a manager who was destined to achieve fame as a lawyer and executive in very high places. The boys sat on my bed and hearing what I had to say, believed it. We were of one mind in that room. The closest friend of my college days was with me again and again as though to keep me firm in my conviction, as though determined to pour his strength into every part of my weakness.

And in adding validity to my answer, not the least of those who came was the doctor himself. His tongue was not in his cheek when at last he gave assent to my decision. He brought more than pills to give me that final lift.

That was the community and the environment in which I prayed to my first answer. "Easy," you say. I think so. Definitely yes!

How difficult it could have been and how different it is now in many institutions of higher learning! Surely scholarship was not less distinguished when Harvard, Yale, Columbia, Dartmouth, Princeton and all the others of our most ancient and honored colleges and universities were founded, than in these same cloistered halls it is today. Yet all of these, and many others, were established with a definite and sometimes exclusive religious purpose. As I write this chapter, a debate over the Town Meeting of the Air has concluded in which was discussed the question: "Have the churches failed?" A distinguished university professor of philosophy and an equally distinguished psychiatrist who is director of a clinic supported the affirmative. A famous clergyman and writer and a brilliant young woman, well known as a lecturer and reviewer of books and the mother of two children, supported the negative.

Being a biased listener, I applauded what I regarded as the telling points made by the negative, and in my opinion —though on occasion they had their hands full—they definitely outmatched their opponents. Particularly poignant was the realism of the mother returning to her faith when, with her children asking for the bread of life, she found rationalism and humanism utterly inadequate.

As I listened to this stirring debate, I became increasingly troubled at one point. What chance would the searching student mind in a university classroom have to receive even a partial incentive to consider favorably— if at all—religion and the church, if departments of philosophy are professored by such dynamic, unqualified denial as that voiced by the philosopher. In his second sentence he said, "I shall have to seem to be a kind of village atheist on a national network." To me he "seemed to be" considerably more than that before he got through.

History bears out the negative, I think: namely, that human progress to this hour in all the fields of culture, democracy, interracial and world peace movements are associated with religious faith. There is no blinking the fact that failures are monumental and progress too slow; but religion, with all the handicaps imposed by many *Christians* through the centuries until now, has set the signs upon the road to progress, and through the churches has kept men marching.

Francis E. Clark, founder of Christian Endeavor, the largest Christian youth movement in the world, told me of how the great President Hopkins of Dartmouth called him into the president's office one morning in the early 1870's and talked with him about a young man's purpose and future. Said Dr. Clark, "The president, knowing my background and being intensely religious himself, urged me to consider, along with other professions and callings, the Christian ministry; and then before he dismissed me, he knelt with me and prayed that I might be led aright." Dr. Clark added, "I am sure that President Hopkins prayed me into my life's work that day!" There was a time when many another college president did as much as that for many another young man—nor has the practice altogether ceased. Such colleges and such college presidents may still be found, though definitely they are not as numerous as they once were.

Dr. Scott, who had retired from the presidency of Ohio State University before I entered there for special graduate work, was my teacher in philosophy. He was a scholar, a clergyman, and a royal friend. He was mentally alert in his ninety-fifth year when he died as the result of an automobile accident. He took me through Kant's *Critique of Pure Reason* and brought me out a more intelligent and, I believe, a more earnest Christian than I was when I entered there with him. He too was a man of prayer, and he had Peace with Power.

The value and strength to each individual and to the group itself of corporate prayer, united prayer, prayer by the group, can hardly be appaised. Let any person tell you of his or her family altar, or remember now your own family altar, and you will add here all that I would write and more. Also psychology must stand thoughtfully, respectfully before the family altar of the Christian home and, indeed, of every other home where prayer is made. But here again, as in personal and private prayer, united prayer beginning as an inheritance must become in your generation and mine and in your home and in my home a present-tense reality, a living experience.

77

The father of Fredric March was an elder in the Presbyterian Church, and the family altar was the central fact of that home's life. The memory of that altar and the inheritance from it are vital influences in the career of this great screen and stage star. But the altar he and Mrs. March (Florence Eldridge) have established is their own experience and that of their children. For the March family here and now, though that first altar has made its worthy contribution, this second altar is for each of them and for their family together, the road to Peace with Power.

Corporate prayer is being employed in these disturbed times when the world rocks as perhaps never before in the history of organized society. The United Nations has set aside a room for prayer, or meditation, or silence. Groups of laymen, prominent labor and industrial leaders, are praying together for peace among nations and between racial and economic groups within nations. Not even a dynamic, publicly professed atheism that fairly shouts "I do not pray" has retarded this rising tide of petition and supplication. Rather, denial and even opposition have accelerated the pace and widened the scope.

Prayer groups meet early in the morning in centrally located rooms in practically every American city, and there are at least two of these groups meeting regularly in the Capitol building in Washington, D. C.

United States Senator Homer Ferguson of Michigan introduced a bill during the second session of the 80th Congress asking for proclamation of Memorial Day as a day of national prayer for peace. We may not have as many Dartmouth presidents praying at their desks with college undergraduates, but there is a rising temperature in prayer circles of the world today, and the promise "Ask and it shall be given you" is being remembered and claimed by unnumbered millions of every race, faith, and condition.

XII

Immortal Until Work Is Done

It would be quite possible to place in a book like this an overemphasis upon life continuing beyond the grave, or rather to emphasize tomorrow at the expense of today. This life is good. God made it. To disregard it, to belittle it, to disparage it even for Heaven, whether in pious phrases or by bringing it to a violent end, is bad for man and evil before God.

To journey is often better than to arrive, anticipation often happier than realization. I knew a wise and happy man whose philosophy included something of each of these. He was nearly ninety when we met, and for another five years we were friends. He contributed much to my ministry, and fellowship with him was mental and spiritual renewal. His spirit was such that young people especially were drawn to him. He was a talented musician, and at fifteen was playing a great organ in a downtown New York church. He founded the New York Philharmonic and until he died was a patron of the Metropolitan Opera. For years he was vice president of a major bank, and at his death he was still president of the American Bible Society. He had made more than a hundred Atlantic crossings and was the senior and most distinguished passenger of the Cunard Line. One evening when we sat together, I asked him the obvious question: "Elder, tell me—what is your secret? You have lived nearly a century and you are still one of the most youthful men I know."

When E. Francis Hyde settled into his chair, smiled, and began to talk, I knew that I was in for a rare experience, but how rare, how really wonderful an experience, I could not know. He began: "Domine, I never reminisce!" He laughed then and began to reminisce, but I had his point. *He did not live in the past.* He had his memories, but he did not live in them. They traveled with him, but always his face was front and he was on the march.

With that beginning, Francis Hyde went on to share with me, as I am sure few if any others ever heard it, the story of his life. Particularly I was interested in what he said about companionship with his wife, whom I had never known. Without what he told me that night, this chapter would not be written.

He said, "For nearly fifty years we spent practically all our summers abroad. I would take Mrs. Hyde to London in June, stay with her for two weeks, return to New York for business, leaving her there, and then go back for another two weeks or longer, after which we would come home together. We traveled in Europe with our

London hotel as headquarters. She loved a horse and we rode together in Hyde Park." He smiled reminiscently before he added, "Until our joints stiffened, and then we took a carriage."

My friend went on quietly with something in his voice now that kept me at even closer attention. "You know I have followed the eclipse over the globe and the year before Mrs. Hyde died—four years before you came—the total was in the Philippines. Mrs. Hyde shook her head. 'No, Francis, I'm not going,' she said. 'But you run along and see your eclipse and I'll go on ahead to London where I shall be comfortable—and happy waiting for you.'" The old man sat silent for a long minute before he finished. "And so I saw the eclipse and headed for London. I crossed the China Sea and rounded India; I sailed up the Indian Ocean and the Red Sea (Oh, was it hot!); I came through the Suez Canal and the blue Mediterranean, by the Gates of Hercules and past the Bay of Biscay into the English Channel. I found her waiting for me. Domine, that will always be the most wonderful journey of my life —*save one*. I did not hurry the trip, though I did not delay it either. I just took it as it came and got the most out of it I could while I reveled in my thoughts of reunion in London. And when I got to London, she was there!" Now I had his secret, and as he searched my face with his still keen and always kindly eyes, he knew that I had it. "Yes —yes," and he nodded his head. "It is like that now. I am journeying toward her, sailing again the seas that lead always to *her*. I have work to do, interesting things to enjoy, and life is good and always she is waiting. I would not hasten the event, Domine. She would be disappointed in me. But I await the hour of reunion; that will be very wonderful. I am ready!"

A few months after that memorable night, when they went to call him in the morning, E. Francis Hyde wasn't there. For him it was reunion.

To live like that is good living. I believe that it is within your choice and mine to be immortal until our work is done. Also I believe that a man may take his life into his own hands, interrupt the divine plan for his life, and shorten his career. Someone has said: "When a life is set to God's plan for it and held there, its time schedule is kept in Heaven." Is that fatalism? Definitely not, for I may still "interrupt the divine plan."

Let me pray then—and I do—to complete the work that is mine to finish. To have strength and courage, faith and time to get it done—well done—and to live no longer than that—please! Nor am I nor are you ever competent to pass the final judgment upon either work or the workman. Length of years and number of days, these are not the measure of a lifetime of service.

Jesus was thirty-three when He was crucified. Lincoln was sixty-four when he was shot.

But faith that prayer commands your future and controls, or may control, your earthly destiny is vastly reassuring. This is a potent faith. Actually you may live as long as you want to! Even a man who professes to have no faith in prayer is likely to agree that here is something that may be a constructive philosophy for daily living. Those who have it will not sit out their days anticipating disaster or plan their course in life just to avoid risk and danger. It is those who sit who have disaster fall upon them and those who chart their course to miss dangers generally run head on into them.

Many a life has backed up into misadventure.

I shall fly, or drive, or sail in ships, or ride on trains as time requires and schedules make necessary to finish the work undone, for always I shall know that God keeps my time if I keep myself in the line of duty and that I shall live as long as I want to!

But some have lived longer than that and here enters the mystery, here is one of the questions we must "hang up" until there is time enough to find their answers.

Have there been times when I believed, when I *knew* that God was stepping in to keep me in time and space? Yes. But does that not show God to be a God of "special interests," granting to some favors that are withheld from others? No—the prayer I pray may be your prayer too, and that of every other person. Every good I know is for each and for all. This is the story of my faith, but it is a formula that may be yours. Also others who died when I survived may well have reached the time that I shall reach, the time when the life task—however humble—is finished, and when that which is better may be claimed.

On some flight or journey or in some quiet place my work shall be finished and then no prayer of mine would grant me an extension of time—nor would I pray that prayer!

A few months ago a letter from a young mother in Virginia who was dying with an incurable disease strangely moved me. She wanted life because of her small children, her husband, her home. Not selfishly did she pray; rather she felt herself to be selfish because her thought of dying was for herself radiant with happiness. However she had come to believe that prayer could and would heal her. It has. At any rate, given up by her doctors and her case pronounced hopeless, she is out of bed and carrying the full burden of her motherhood.

You may remember the words of the distinguished physicist Alexis Carrel: "Those occasions . . . when prayer has overcome the so-called laws of nature, the occasions when prayer has dramatically done this have been termed miracles." The day after Dr. Carrel retired from his relationships with the Rockefeller Institute I sat with him and with another friend who is a practicing physician in New York City. During the luncheon conversation Dr. Carrel said that twice he had seen cancer "crystallize and disappear" when the result could be traced only to prayer.

Tragic it is that seldom indeed do they "crystallize and disappear." Guarded must be our claims. Nor should we make claims beyond His will for those who, in the line of duty and with faith that is stronger than Carrel's "so-called laws of nature," experience His healing. But *always* you may be immortal until your work is done.

More than forty years ago William Wright, a young man of Salem, Ohio, only recently married, went to Crile's Clinic in Cleveland. An exploratory operation revealed a malignancy that could not be removed. The opening was closed and my friend came home to die. But he said, *"I am not going to die,"* and he seemed to know. He convinced his wife, his friends, his immediate community. These forty years in which William Wright has fathered children, rejoiced in his grandchildren, achieved success in business, and rendered a constant service to his community and through his church to the world prove that William Wright is immortal until his work is done.

And in my life, too, there have been a few "coincidences" —or something more. The trip into the remote Siletz Basin of Oregon when, with no medical aid to be had, I all but died with "inflammation of the bowels," which was no doubt acute appendicitis with a ruptured appendix; the field in France where twice under a close-up barrage in World War I I was uninjured; and a bank of the Upper Rhine in World War II when, under direct fire of a "pill box" not a hundred yards away, I was unhurt. All that I could do was pray that prayer for others as for myself. Pray in terror, yes, but believing. Do you say, "Also there with you, and thousands of times elsewhere, men escaped when conditions were even worse"? The answer is "Yes— certainly." Twice I have missed planes that went on to fatal landings, and once an elevator crashed in Columbus with fatal results—an elevator whose door was open as it waited for me when I was called to my office. But again you say, "Others—millions of them—have stories and coincidences even more startling." Again the answer is, "Yes—certainly."

And here let it be written that there is a temptation to be resisted, an evil to be avoided, in acknowledging the amazing grace that God the Infinite releases to you and to me who are finite. That evil is pride, and the temptation is the temptation to fall into the mood of the Pharisee's thanksgiving. You will remember that he thanked God that he was not as other men, even as the publican who knelt in humility, crying out his unworthiness.

This story of my faith, my experience in prayer—

prayer that through the years of my life, in the daily affairs with which I have been charged, has given me Peace with Power—must be, and is equally, a confession of weakness and failure, of too little done and too many mistakes made when the resources available were limitless and the promise infinite.

The very title selected for this book by its publishers is presumptuous and can be justified only if what I have written helps those who read to find what I have found, but to use it better—helps them experience even more fully that which is for me glorious beyond words but still just a beginning.

XIII

A Personal God

MY FRIEND SAID, "You don't believe in a personal God? Really now!"

"But I do," I replied. "To me, God is as real and as personal as you!" And then I shared with him my experience. "Once I thought of God as a *particular person*," I said, and I told him of the old Bible with the picture of an angry deity driving Adam and Eve from the Garden of Eden, and of how I reacted to the picture. God, as *that* person, was cruel and hateful; I wanted none of him, though I feared Him. But God, with all the attributes of personality and with personality lifted into creative power and authority; God all-wise, all-powerful, all-knowing; God of infinite love and forgiveness; God fully revealed in Jesus Christ—in Him I not only believe, but to Him I pray, and from Him I have the answer to my prayer.

My friend understood; he sensed the difference. Indeed, his own experience was similar to mine. The God he

feared as a little boy was a bearded man standing at a
tall desk and writing in a book. The names of the good
and of the bad were being written there, and punishments
and rewards were being assigned. "The old man's back
was toward me," my friend said. "I had an almost un-
controllable desire to try for a glance over his shoulder,
but I was afraid—afraid that my name would be on the
wrong side of the ledger." He, too, thought of God as a
particular person, and a quite terrible person.

I went on from there to tell my friend, as I have already
written in this book, just how Jesus Christ had become to
me the very experience of God, of how to me Jesus Christ
is God, and without Him I would have no God. I pray to
Jesus Christ, and when I pray to Him I pray to God; or,
if you prefer, I pray to God in the name of and through
Jesus Christ.

And when God answers, always Jesus Christ is speaking.

There is one important caution that I accept for myself, even as I enter it here. There is a stern, unyielding,
and self-righteous "orthodoxy" that judges others by the
tests applied to oneself and then adds: "Thus saith the
Lord." Paul the Apostle wrote: "Who also hath made us
able ministers of the New Testament, not of the letter,
but of the spirit, for the letter killeth, but the spirit giveth
life."

I may not and I do not apply to others the "letter" of
that which I accept for myself. God speaks to each even as
He speaks to all. Men may not have time or the dis-
position to listen, but He speaks!

There is for you, as for me, His personal message, and I

may share with you *only* that which I have experienced—
that which, not in the particulars perhaps, but in the
formula "Ask and it shall be given you," will surely open
for you the way to Peace with Power.

Life, life, more life, is the hunger cry of the soul, and
it is not the "letter" but the "spirit," not the law but the
fulfillment of the law, that gives life. Jesus said that He
came not to destroy the law but to fulfill the law, not to
fulfill the law in forms and institutions but in men and
women, by setting them free of their sins and fears, their
taboos and hates, by equipping them in body and soul to
live the *abundant* life here and now.

At least nine-tenths of all the recorded activities of
Jesus have to do directly with the physical, the bodily
needs of people; and remember, the schedule of Jesus is
the pattern of God!

Jesus acted as though He believed that He got men and
women ready for Heaven when He prepared and made
them fit to live with their fellow men in the world. Also
He acted as though His spiritual message, His food for
the soul, should wait until the body's hunger had been
satisfied or its sickness cured.

My friend has found God to be very personal. Now he
prays as he was never able to pray before, and God answers. There would be no reason to pray, no justification
for a prayer, if God were not personal, as real and personal as the parent to whom we turn in confidence, but
vastly more able to answer the cry of our need.

Do you have, as eventually I had, difficulty in accepting
the fact of a God able or concerned enough to turn aside
from making worlds to give attention to one small voice?

That almost stopped me as the implication grew upon me. Two billion human beings in the world now, and countless billions before and after. What a bedlam, to say the least!

It would be easy to dismiss the whole matter with the airy wave of a hand and a "Faith is the answer," or "With God all things are possible." And of course faith is the answer and all things are possible with God, and believing and accepting—these are sum and substance of the whole vast matter.

But I found something more—nothing greater, to be sure; nor was it comparable to these—yet it helped me comprehend and accept their truth. It helped make truth come alive in me.

When I was a child I lived in a very small community, one of the earliest trading centers of the Oregon country. I was less than two years old when I came to it and have no knowledge of things seen before. My first recollection of trains has to do with a whistle that, when the wind was right, I could clearly hear. An older and wiser lad told me that Indians riding over great wheels made the train go and that the whistle was the war whoop dedicated to peace. To a very small boy, it was a thrilling explanation.

When, one never-to-be-forgotten day, my father took me to meet the train, I was nearly frantic with excitement. I saw first the smoke that rose behind the trees that rimmed the horizon. Then I heard the war whoop, and then out from the forest it came—an amazing thing—little houses chasing each other across a field with the smoking kitchen in front!

The world that I first knew and now remember was

A PERSONAL GOD

like that. There were less than two hundred people in it,
with other people more remote, from whom letters came,
and once a yellow envelope that Father called a "telegram." I knew all these people—men, women, and children. That was my world.

Then I went away. Now, after many years, my world
has grown until it includes the continents, the islands, and
the oceans of the earth, with "the inhabitants thereof." As
I write, I am conscious of people in practically every
major community and in unnumbered small places over
the world. I think of Singapore, Algiers, Helsinki, Tokyo,
Manila, Capetown, Cairo, Budapest, London, Madrid,
Paris, Berlin, Stockholm, Peiping, Timbuktu, Brisbane,
Java, Bombay, the villages of China and Kashmir—but
my fingers tire. And when I think of these capitals and
towns, I see faces—the faces and forms of those I know;
I think of my friends.

It is a long call from Lafayette, Oregon, in 1887 to
Philadelphia and New York in 1950, and from two hundred people to all of these. It is a long call from the war
whoop and the little houses chasing a kitchen across a
field to the giant ships in which I have flown around the
world. Faith cannot be rationalized and you cannot reduce
the experience of prayer and its answers to the residue
found in a crucible. God is Infinite, and infinitely more
than any test tube demonstrates. But it is easier now for
me to understand how it all could be. Lift what I have
come to know, what my finite mind has achieved and my
human heart experienced to some infinite degree, and you
come to the experience of prayer and prayers answered.

Starting with the experience, you reach, even in reason,

the intimation of how and why the Infinite God is both able and concerned enough to turn aside from making worlds to give attention to one small voice. If God is personal—as I have found Him to be—and if like begets like, how else than from personality could personalities derive? If God is personal, then surely He would wish to own the person created in His image, made to think with Him and after Him.

Jesus said, "If ye then being evil [limited, inadequate, human—all that the word implies] know how to give good gifts unto your children, how much more shall your Father which is in Heaven give good things to them that *ask* Him?"

Though the experience of prayer and prayers answered transcends reason and is beyond rationalization, it is for me now the most reasonable thing in the world. But though prayer has an "explanation" in science, as the greatest scientists now affirm, and has become the vehicle of psychologists and psychiatrists, it is beyond these. Where science must still tarry and stop, prayer marches straight to the throne of God.

This is the reason, the infallible reason, why prayer is always answered and why it is the road to Peace with Power.

XIV

Prayer Is Power over Practical Affairs

MY PATERNAL GRANDFATHER was born in Virginia. He became, when very young, a circuit rider with a parish that was anchored on the Potomac River and swung then across Western Pennsylvania and Eastern Ohio to Lake Erie. His hardships and sacrifices were second only to those of his wife, the amazing woman he left behind to keep his home and mother his eight children while he rode the wilderness, crossing rivers and mountains to preach and minister to the ever westward-moving pioneers.

I have heard him repeat from the ancient scriptures one passage that in the days of his hardships and poverty was his pillow text for the log cabin he left behind and his comfort when he bedded down his horse and rolled into his blankets under a great tree: "I have been young and now I am old; yet have I not seen the righteous forsaken nor his seed begging bread."

Grandmother had her memories too, and she would

95

smile when he recited the verse, smile and nod and sometimes add, "Father is right. It was so—even when the
salary he didn't get was seventy-five dollars a year!" Her
hands, with those of the children, made up the deficit. The
garden, the cow, the pigs, and the orchard were the gran-
ary. I have seen the stumps of the trees he planted between
missions, and that the family pruned and tended, and from
which they gathered the harvests at last. My father, his
son, claimed the promise of the same great word. When
I first became acquainted with him, he was supporting a
family of nine children on four hundred dollars a year—
when he was fortunate enough to receive the money. I
remember my sense of affluence when Father's salary went
to six hundred a year. I wondered what we would do with
the extra money. But the man who sired me was a finan-
cier—or rather, Mother was! No, it was an inspired
partnership, and again the woman's flying hands and fighting heart supplemented the income. Nor were we forsaken, and we never begged. Somehow, too, every child
who lived to the age of going, went to college, though
Father had to found one college and preside over the
destiny of another to get us all through.

We children were taught to pray for wisdom and guidance, for direct help too in practical, every-day matters;
and the example of our parents gave us what was, perhaps, a childlike faith. But never did those prayers for
Heaven's aid conclude without the acceptance of the
responsibility for getting busy to get the answer to the
prayer. "Pray without ceasing and work accordingly" was
one of Father's mottoes, and one of his favorite texts
was: "Faith without works is dead."

96

Among the last conversations with Father was one in which, reminiscing, he smiled as he talked of his parents and their firm reliance upon God to supply "all wants" according to the formula of "ask" and "go out for it." He added this: "My son, remember that promise and remember that to your father and his father and to others before them the promise never failed—your mother and I had more when she went on ahead than at any other time in our lives, and you children—well, you've never had to beg bread or anything else since you stopped pestering for candy or ribbons long ago."

It was in this atmosphere that my prayer life began, and my prayer inheritance had in it very practical particulars. Nor has the prayer experience of the accumulating years lessened this quality—or decreased the quantity! Isaiah's prayer, too, has become increasingly mine: For the "all things" of life "I will trust and not be afraid." And I find that when I trust I am not afraid.

When we discovered that two were presently to become three in our house, my salary was five hundred dollars for the year, only one hundred dollars more than Father's, but I got mine. We prayed, and then I went down to southern Ohio and borrowed the money to make a reception for our first-born son. Today I wonder how I ever repaid the loan, but it was paid.

Then came a time when the house we owned had to be sold, sold within a stated time, sold to avoid great embarrassment. Everything possible had been done, but even our everything was not enough, and it was Saturday before the Monday! Would we be able to sell it in time? I had prayed before, but now the prayer took on propor-

97

tions, became of the Jacob quality by the brook Jabok. That night the buyer came and fairly tore the property out of my hands.

After that, conditions bettered for us. We had a lovely farm in New England and there were horses in the barn. Those horses were my dream come true. I do not remember when I first rode. Father once remarked in disgust, "You would think you were born on a horse." But Mother had the answer for that one. "Well he wasn't," she said and smiled.

But the two Morgans in their stalls were too heavy a load to carry when the depression came, and so to keep the children in school, we took the horses out of their stalls. Then came the dark day when we had to offer the farm for sale. "Long House" went on the block. The children were wonderful. Children always are in a family crisis. Oldsters crack before their youngsters do. We had stripped the place, or thought we had, to the bone. Then to pay taxes, I sold timber—hardwood, oak, and maple I had vowed never to part with. But we could not sell the place. We dropped the price, dropped it again. Prospects came, looked, and turned away. We forgot price and sought an offer—any offer. Other properties sold. All about us transfers were made. But Long House, so right for our large family of eight children, and for all the children of our friends in distant lands, was just too big for anyone not interested in an institution, and during that depression, you couldn't give such a property as ours to an institution.

But you say, "Why didn't you pray? That should have been another easy one for you!" No, these crises have not been easy. Nothing is easy that bends you to your knees. And we did pray—how constantly we prayed *to sell*!

Well, the answer came, but not the answer that we asked for, not our answer. The 1936 hurricane was the answer, and if you try to embarrass me with the question, "Why does God send or allow hurricanes and the like," I reply again that there are questions we must "hang up" and let hang until there will be time enough. However, the scientists may have a partial answer for the question: there are physical and natural compensations even for hurricanes.

That hurricane pushed over one of the finest stands of white pine, spruce, and hemlock in southern New Hampshire. Four days of rain before the Big Blow came had soaked the earth and loosened the ground so that those great mushrooms of rootage fell an easy victim of the unprecedented storm.

Nothing but that "Act of God" could have persuaded me to sell those trees. They were my pride and joy. It would have been a "sin" not to spare them, and no mortal hand tore them from the sky. But the sale of that uprooted timber provided the final fund that got us *His* answer for our prayer, and today Long House is still— and, please God, evermore shall be—ours.

Now our grandchildren are beginning where their parents left off, and life is even more wonderful than it was before. Presently the grandchildren will bring their friends to the New Hampshire hills as our children brought theirs.

As I have reread the lines of this chapter, it all sounds so simple—no, not that, not simple, but self-sufficient,

99

which would be even less true to the facts of the case. Of course, when we turned to "ask," we acknowledged that we were not sufficient, and when having done our dead level best, we fell so far short of being able to meet our crises, then we knew that we were not self-sufficient.

But again and again God's hand, reaching to us and lifting us up and over, was the familiar hand of a friend, of a man or a woman we knew and loved and trusted. The ancient scripture reads: "I have not seen the righteous forsaken nor his seed begging bread," but so often there have been those who stood for God and supplied the "bread" or its equivalent. There are a few special names—very special—I shall whisper in the Great Companion's ear when I meet Him in the morning.

"Ask and it shall be given you" is His promise and He is not limited to direct intervention when He goes about keeping His promise. Also, when He moves through His agents on the earth His "wonders to perform," wonders small as well as great, wonders that keep even one humble family together, the alchemy of His love and grace may create within the recipients of his "miracles" the will and means to perform other miracles for Him—and to know the joy of the performance. And so again, prayer becomes the road to Peace with Power.

XV

Prayer and Power to Heal

My first prayer to an answer was definitely a prayer for recovery from illness, a prayer for physical healing, and I shall return to that theme and amplify it in this chapter.

On July 4, 1921, with Mrs. Poling, our eldest daughter, and our two sons, I was driving from Lake Sunapee in New Hampshire to New York City. That evening an International Christian Endeavor Convention, the details of which had been in my hands, was opening in the Armory on Park Avenue at 34th Street. Between Greenfield and Northampton in Massachusetts, the steering rod pulled out of the "knuckle," and the automobile, a touring car with a soft top, crashed into a telephone pole and turned over.

The road was clear and perfectly straight at the point of the crash, but I had slowed my speed because some children were playing with fire-crackers in front of a house just ahead of us. When I was directly in front of the children and passing them, I turned the wheel to bring the car again into the middle of the highway and accelerated. It was then that things happened! I had the sensation of that wheel loose in my hands and spinning. Instinctively I looked down. Then at the startled cry of Mrs. Poling, I looked up and saw the pole directly ahead. It was too late to swerve. There was open road ahead and a flat tobacco field at our left, but we chose the pole— there was nothing I could do. Later, when our son Clark was visited in the hospital by his uncle, he observed to the boy that a few inches would have landed us all quite comfortably in the tobacco field. With a characteristic wink and grin, Clark replied, "But, Uncle, you know how Dad does hate tobacco!"

When the heavy car met the pole as it overturned, it swung to the right and all but the driver were thrown clear. I was caught between the seat back, which broke off, and the instrument board. The wheel splintered and ran by my groin.

Mrs. Poling went through the windshield. Her right ear was all but severed, and she was deeply bruised. Remarkable surgery has left her with scarcely a sign.

Our daughter was thrown into the road and received face burns which became infected. She was a real sufferer before she was sound again, but today there is not a scar.

The boys were more severely hurt. In addition to the shock we all experienced, the elder had a serious break in the shoulder and the younger in the hip. The break in the hip did not yield until it had been set and rebroken several times; then through super-heated July and August days the boy lay between sand bags with his left leg suspended from the ceiling. But in the end he and his brother too made complete recoveries, and the arm helped win football and basketball games and equaled a scholastic record in the pole vault. That left leg of the younger lad was supplemented at first by a crutch and a shoe lift, then a crutch with a lift; finally even the lift was discarded. Presently the leg, perhaps stronger than its mate, was helping make football history.

Since I was at the wheel, my experience was naturally more severe. When the car came down upon me, I did not lose consciousness completely, thanks to my wife. She came to me. She forced her way back under the machine, pressed her lips against my ear, and called my name. Called and called and did not cease calling my name, staccato and insistent, until men who were providently at hand lifted the car and carried me out.

I heard that voice—how clearly I remember after these years—as though it came out to me at the end of the world and from very far away. Instinctively I knew that I must keep on hearing it. Ages it seemed, though actually only seconds passed. Once I felt so comfortable that I almost stopped listening, but the voice called me back, would not let me go. Later in the hospital I was told that had ever I stopped listening, I would have died; but I knew as much before they told me.

An inventory of my body made by Dr. Hansen revealed two fractures in the vertebrae, three fractured ribs, crushed hips, a crushed breast bone, a wounded head, and unpredictable internal injuries. For ten days no one could do anything but wait. The doctors knew what they were waiting for, or thought they did, but two of us knew something better! We had *from the beginning the absolute assurance of recovery, not merely of life, but of recovery.*

I made it clear—we made it clear—that we "asked" recovery, and the answer came clear and without conditions attached: "Recovery." I never doubted nor even questioned until actual danger was past, when I wavered just a little. Weakness or weariness it may have been. But *she* never wavered. She is like that.

Again I was fortunate in my physician. Dr. Hansen had learned in World War I what Nature does when left completely to herself. He co-operated with Nature. For days, there could be no question, even, about the wisdom of an operation on the vertebrae, or a brace for the back; but later when the specialists from New York and Boston insisted on surgery and Mrs. Poling and I said "No," Dr. Hansen said "No" with us. We stood together, and perhaps the doctor stood first. There is no further need of the story. All that matters is told. My recovery was and is complete. That back has carried me over the world and become stronger after the crash than it had been before. Not a scar from that ordeal remains anywhere visible in our family, and "Asking" did it!

Once when in my hospital room the specialists were looking at the "pictures," I said, "Either the pictures are wrong or something more potent than surgery took over."

Dr. Hansen turned and smiled. "The pictures aren't wrong, Poling!" he replied. But even so, he played a vital part in my case and the family's. We shall never be able to repay him, never adequately express our gratitude.

That complete healing was a long drawn-out affair. I learned to walk again. You may not remember when and how you learned to walk. I do. Gripping the foot of the hospital bed firmly with my right hand and with my left arm over the doctor's strong shoulder, again and again I lowered my feet until I touched the floor. Again and again I swung my limbs from the old bruised hips, making the motions of walking. Finally I dropped a fraction, just a fraction, of a pound of my weight onto my feet on the floor. It was agony. But it passed. Then came a year in the Southwest—a wonderful year for us all—and then life in full stride again!

I have referred in a previous chapter to the compensations, but they can never be told or even fully remembered. Again I write that I would never have chosen the ordeal, but never shall I cease to be grateful for what is mine and ours out of it. Life would be an almost empty thing were the riches coming from that accident to be taken away.

But the prayer that made me whole, while it was a united prayer, *our* prayer, was also chiefly the prayer of Lillian, my wife. There is a direct promise to cover such a case as this: "The Prayer of Faith shall save the sick." That promise came true in me and in mine. It was a healing not without medical assistance and care, but with medical assistance and care—*and also beyond them.*

That promise, "The Prayer of Faith shall save the sick," has been made the excuse and occasion of charlatans and other designing people. Perhaps the Church, the Protestant Church particularly, in recent times has neglected this healing ministry that had so large and honorable a place in the Early Church—neglected and even abandoned it because of the abuses that crept in. There is no excuse for this neglect. There are increasing signs that the Churches generally are returning to that Promise.

The growth of Christian Science, Unity, and other similar groups is confirmation of the greater fact that "the Great Physician still is nigh," that Jesus Christ who healed in Judea and Galilee heals here and now, that God is not baffled by even our "incurables," but is the same yesterday, today, and forever.

Only a few times in my own ministry have I been impelled to appeal in prayer for an abrupt decision in a sickness, and then only when there was an irresistible "leading."

Once in Canton, Ohio, I came into a home of great poverty. A little boy lay unconscious with pneumonia. Crying out with every breath, he seemed to be dying. The doctor had done everything he could and gone away. The young mother cried out to me as the father held her and tried to comfort her. It was the second year of my ministry, but I felt as I had never felt before that prayer would "save the sick." With my hand upon that fairly steaming brow, I prayed. . . . He seemed to grow better immediately! And he lived.

That recovery was presently an embarrassment to the young preacher. The incident became a series of "recoveries" as it was told and retold in the community. I was in danger of being regarded as a professional faith healer, a practicing specialist. And never was I that. Indeed I never was "led" to be that. Mary, the mother of Jesus, said to His Disciples at the marriage in Canaan of Galilee, "Whatsoever He sayeth unto thee, do it!" And that has been the word I have always waited for.

I do not question those other sincere and more competent operators in this vast field of needy men and women. *Rather, I envy them.* But save only in such a restricted and limited way, it has never been granted me. Perhaps God has had other things for me to do.

Twice in acute sickness, when my wife was desperately ill, I have known that God was ready to release healing power through me. In each instance we were on a transcontinental train, the need was immediate and imperative, and "no other help was nigh." Once the crisis came between Portland and Klamath Falls in Oregon; once as we traveled between Pocatello, Idaho, and Cheyenne, Wyoming. Each time excruciating pain was relieved under my hand and as I prayed. Each time the recovery was complete and the indications of conditions requiring a major surgical operation disappeared.

But generally, and far more frequently, prayer has opened doors of activity or opportunity that have enabled us to find the cure, or made entrances through which we have passed to meet the competent physician. Once in Peiping, China, in December, 1935, after a second gall bladder seizure that in Shanghai two weeks before had all but persuaded us to accept the diagnosis and submit Mrs. Poling to the operation, we were turned away from one great institution. It was Saturday, after hours, and the attendant could not be made to understand the emergency. No one was to blame.

A missionary friend hurried with us to the German Embassy Compound where we found the great Dr. Krieg just leaving the Embassy hospital. Already he was beyond his time. He was gruff and typically German, but when Mrs. Poling spoke in German and when I told him that the other hospital would not admit us after hours, he took us in! There we found a new culture, produced in German laboratories between the wars, that was, I think, responsible for my wife's recovery and that started her toward sound health. She has never had that operation! Again and again, with us, with intimate friends, one of whom was with us on a journey around the world, the prayer of faith has "saved the sick" in such a manner, rather than by direct action. God seems to want us to play our part, to do our full share, to use the skill and cures that men have acquired and discovered. But for me it is still the prayer of faith that saves the sick and leads to Peace with Power.

XVI

Prayer and the Church

O NE SUNDAY NIGHT years ago a man of distinguished appearance came to me at the close of a Sunday evening service in my New York City church. He had raised his hand in response to the simple invitation that with little variation I have extended at the close of practically every sermon I have preached at home and abroad during more than thirty years. This is the invitation: "If there are those here who have burdens too great for them to bear alone—whatever the burden—sin, fear, sickness, doubt— *whatever the burden,* if *you* are here and would be remembered in my closing brief prayer, you may stand or lift your hand and I shall see you and pray for you." Before extending that invitation always I ask the congregation to bow for prayer so that my invitation is to a silent, *unseeing* congregation.

On the occasion referred to, the gentleman who had come to meet me—and always that invitation follows the other—said with cynicism in his voice, "Well, what can you do for me?"

"Nothing," I replied, "absolutely nothing, but I can take you to One who will answer your question."

We spent some time together that night, and during the following week we met twice. At the close of the second meeting when we had prayed together, the man said, "Listen to me! How does it happen that because years ago I made a promise, I've been going to church at least once every week, but until last Sunday night I was never invited to do anything about it?"

My simple ministry has been based upon the belief that the supreme business of the Christian Church is leading men and women to Jesus Christ, sustaining and strengthening them in the Christian life, training them for and engaging them in Christian service. And this program is always a blood brother to social and community service.

But to build a new world we must first have new builders. If the leadership of the Christian Church has learned only one lesson well in a generation of being busy about many things, it is this: Redemption is decisively more than intellectual interpretation; private and corporate sin more than a name; atonement more than a theory; and Jesus as the Christ more than a myth.

The simple invitation that my pulpit extends is based upon three assumptions: 1.) In every congregation and group there are those who need and desire God; 2.) God's Spirit is always active and always God is there! 3.) The least I should do and all I may do is to make it possible for those who need God, who need a faith to live by and who want Peace with Power, to meet the One and Only One who is able here and now to give them what they need and want. *It is just as simple as that.*

There are some who call this "following the line of least resistance" and say that it is too simple. Definitely I try to follow the line of least resistance, and if the whole thing is "simple," then I am happy, for Jesus was like that. The common people "heard him gladly" for that very reason—they could understand him. The great David James Burrell once said, "Simplicity is rock crystal; profundity is mud!"

In the more than thirty years that invitation has failed only once of bringing a response. That night of failure came in the first year and I know why I failed, for it was my failure.

Among the most pregnant words of Jesus and His most characteristic invitation was "Come and see." He invited those who followed Him with their questions to look into the matter for themselves. He never insulted the intelligence of His hearers nor talked down to them. He respected their minds, regarded their personalities, as well as ministered to their hungry and suffering bodies. Come and see for yourselves, He said. Watch Me at work. Study My methods, see what happens, know for yourselves, and then decide for yourselves. He did not coerce men's minds; rather, on merit, He persuaded and won them. Then, of course, He commanded their allegiance; those who had "seen" Him followed Him through dangers, hardships, and human disasters to the death. But they knew what they were doing and, knowing, they would do no other. That which held them was not mailed might but sacrificial love.

How entirely apart from the personality and message

of the one extending the invitation the timelessness of the invitation itself may be, I have seen demonstrated repeatedly. On one occasion, following a citizenship address in a regular Sunday service, but to a special audience, I was strongly tempted to pronounce the benediction without extending the ·invitation. Subconsciously, as I spoke—it *must* have been a subconscious thought—I prayed for guidance. I got the guidance. I extended the invitation and more than fifty men and women responded.

Twenty-five years ago, among those whom I met at the close of my New York service was a young man who did not give me his name. He stated that he did not desire an interview; said that he had been attending my services for three months; that several times he had accepted my invitation and raised his hand; now he wished me to know that he felt the need of being remembered in a very special way. Two weeks later the young man came to me again and asked for a personal interview. We met on the next afternoon. I told him, as is my custom, that he need give me no information concerning himself, that the interview was entirely in his hands, and I at his command, but that, of course, my ability to help him would be largely determined by his willingness to trust me. Still he did not give me his name.

Two weeks later he came again and now he gave me his name, a proud name, and told me his story. He had been a combat pilot in World War I under another flag than ours. He was shot down and all but fatally wounded. Scars covered his body. As the result of both physical and nervous demoralization, the after-war period had been for him a time of torture. His was a proud family and he had shamed his people. A long story it was, but now, after twenty-five years, I remember the details. Especially do I remember the "happy ending" that came as through prayer he found Peace with Power and went on to rehabilitate himself. I saw him often until he moved away, and one Christmas Sunday evening I found myself standing face to face with his father and mother. Only those who have lived to experience such an hour can know what that meeting meant to all of us.

My memories have been revived, for after more than twenty years of silence, and as I write this book, I have heard from my friend. He is successful in family life and in business, and the faith he found in a church on a New York avenue has kept him at the source of Power. I look forward to meeting him, and perhaps soon, when I travel to his part of the world.

Not all the experiences of a man's ministry in the church have an ending like that. There are disappointments, disillusionments, and failures; but the average of success is high, for you deal with power that transcends time and space and that only a man's will for his own life can finally defeat.

In these years more than twelve thousand men and women, young and old, have responded to that public invitation, and perhaps no one of these escaped altogether the touch of God's grace upon their lives. At least a few thousand have gone out to live differently, gone out to help answer the preacher's prayer for them that "with God's help tomorrow shall be different than today or yesterday, different and better."

Here is the gamble, the great game of chance that

has made life for me very wonderful. "Take a chance, Preacher!" he said as he stood with bleary, boyish eyes looking at me. He was soaked to the skin, brazenly drunk —and tragically young; that last to me was somehow the important thing. He wanted money and his whole story was impossible. He was the son of wealthy parents; he had fallen among thieves and lost his money—at least that sounded like the prodigal son, and he looked the part. His baggage was being held by the hotel for his unpaid bill. Finally he affirmed that on Tuesday a representative of his family would arrive and fix things up. He needed fifteen dollars, only fifteen, to meet his immediate necessities, and he would repay me on Tuesday without fail.

I knew he was lying and the anxious church officer who knew some of his pastor's weaknesses had started the boy on a swift march for a side door when he turned and blurted out, "Take a chance!" . . . And I did.

What it was that prompted me to give that lad another look I do not know (perhaps the far-reaching power of a mother's prayer), but I did look again and I did take that chance.

The disgust with which the official and my friend received my request to advance the fifteen dollars and charge the same to my personal account was entirely warranted.

Presently the boy went out half-sobered by my parting word. "I've taken the chance," I said, "and a wilder chance it is than any gambler ever took, but, O son, for the sake of many another needy fellow who will come here for help, as well as for your own sake, make good— play the man. Go and God be with you."

The boy came back, came back clean and polished, came back with fifteen dollars, too. Came back to take me to the hotel, where I met a gracious Southern woman who had come in the stead of the boy's invalid mother. The story she told made me weep, but made me glad that I had "taken the chance."

And so through the years they have come and gone, the young, the middle-aged, and the old. Men and women, great sinners and those who were only weak or sinned against. Some have been wise, trained in the schools of America and abroad. Some have come in financial failure and others at the high point of their success. Some have been little people by their own confession, and others have been much smaller than at first they were willing to confess; but all came looking for peace and hoping, hoping sometimes against hope, to find it.

Very soon after I first extended that invitation that was to lead me so far and to so many, I came upon great wisdom. I learned that often, and perhaps generally, those who come to you with questions will find their own answers if you just give them a chance to talk, to speak their questions and problems to a sympathetic listener. I shall not forget one occasion: Two came together. They were husband and wife and he was a professor in a Middle Western state university. Their problem was real and intimate—too intimate to be discussed in their home community. And as I listened, I realized that their problem was quite beyond me. I listened then harder and longer than was my usual custom. That afternoon I discovered that I had been talking too much and too soon. Also I prayed *for myself* that somehow in that room and together we might find the answer. Suddenly—or was it suddenly? Perhaps the solution had been forming all through that conference as they wept and talked and I listened and prayed. But at a moment the answer was there, and they believe—believe to this day—that I was the one who led them to it. I have told them all that I have written here, told them that they more than I deserve gratitude for the results of that conference, but they remain of the same opinion still; and so across a dozen years we have been grateful to each other and in mutual gratitude have found mutual happiness.

XVII

Those Who Prayed with Me

I HAVE WRITTEN of many who prayed with me and who contributed so much to my religious experience. The prayers of others have supplemented my own and strengthened my life for the ministry of the Church and for all other activities with which my life has been associated.

Two men in the ancient New York parish, the oldest Protestant congregation with a continuous history in America, identified themselves with me in prayer. One, a successful real estate operator, was saint-like in his personal life, but dynamic in church affairs as well as in his own operations. No clergyman relied more fully upon prayer and no mystic was more discerning of the spiritual heart of church life. With equal felicity he could conduct a mid-week prayer service, or plan and build a summer camp and home for girls. Once when for weeks he had been exhausted and ill, he sent for me and said, "Well-meaning friends have urged that I have (and he named a clergyman then prominently identified with a faith healing mission) visit me. I do not need any one but my own pastor. Perhaps you will pray for me and with me today." He hesitated then but added, "If you do not object, I wish that as you pray you would put your hand on my head." And so in his room overlooking the Hudson River, with my hand upon his head, I prayed with and for my friend and associate whom I loved and admired. Then presently he was in his familiar place again, and something had been added to our already firm, understanding friendship.

Now to that immortal friendship has been added the continuing friendship of his son, this family's third active generation in the old church. The son, a great engineer serving his country and community in both war and peace, continues the family tradition and is superintendent of the church school.

Elder E. Francis Hyde, whose name has appeared before in this book, was the second of the two men in the New York church during my pastorate who made prayer the center of their careers. One thing I add to what I have already written. For two years I had been trying to persuade my officials to allow me to establish a wayside pulpit at the corner of Fifth Avenue and 29th Street, setting it up within the high iron fence where it could be entered from the south door. We had a wise rule that no major innovation would be added to our program without unanimous action, and that I could not get.

One Sunday evening I found Elder Hyde waiting for me in the study after I had finished greeting those who came into the chancel at the close of the service. "How much did you say it would cost to build and maintain that wayside pulpit through a spring and summer season?" he asked. He knew the answer all right, but I told him again. His gray eyes twinkled as he drew an envelope from his coat pocket saying, "When the Special Work Committee meets this week, you tell *us* that you have the money for that pulpit 'outside the budget' and perhaps we can be persuaded!" And they were. Elder Hyde spoke of the matter after I presented it. He said that he didn't too much like the idea himself, but that the young pastor had a great concern to do it, had been patient about it too, and—well, since the money was available, he felt the pulpit should be tried out for one season at least. The other friend of whom I have written supported Mr. Hyde. I was sure there was collusion, but the entire committee agreed and the Wayside Pulpit, which continued through the years of my ministry, was established.

It is, of course, impossible to put into such a story as this the names of all or even many of those who prayed with and for my ministry, but in Philadelphia again there were two men who stood fast with me in that unique intimacy of prayer. They were my personal friends before I came to be their pastor, and now they became my partners in Service. One, a successful lawyer with practically unnumbered associated interests, is in many aspects the most unusual Christian layman I have ever known. At this writing he is leading counsel for many of the major agencies of his denomination, as well as for similar agencies of other churches. He is a trustee of a theological seminary and its counsel, teacher of a Sunday class of young men that during the war he serviced with a weekly digest of the lesson to every major front of the world. He is president of the State Convention of his Church, but chiefly, and often to the exclusion of all other matters, he is a personal friend and counselor of literally scores of individuals of all ages. The only business I have ever brought him is trouble—and more trouble! Ask me: "What is the secret of this man?" and the answer is "Prayer"; and his second name is Loyalty. No clergyman has ever known a more constant, understanding, helpful friend and associate.

My other Philadelphia example is a credit man, one of the most highly regarded and successful in his city. As to his multiple interests, what I have written about my other friend, who is his friend, applies equally to him. With rare discernment and with intimate understanding of people, he applies to his superintendency of a Sunday School or his chairmanship of an International Christian Endeavor committee the veritable genius in organization that operates in his business. He can be hard as nails, but he is tender and kind, and of all the men I have known, he is the master of the amenities of personal and official relationships. The secret of his life is prayer.

It is baffling to approach even the particulars of one man's work in the Christian Church, for they could not be contained in a library of books, but always those about which I write in this story center in men and women, and always they stand back upon the foundation of prayer.

The women of a parish are the irreducible minimum of its existence and also the hope and assurance of its more abundant life. They charge, and keep charged, the spiritual dynamos; numerically, at least, they constitute the corporate soul of its worship services and they are the Marthas who make its rooms beautiful and who fill it with physical ministries to the community and to the world.

I pay my tribute here in this memory of one woman to all the faithful and inspiring women of the churches I have served. Venerable and queenly, she was the widow of the senior elder who preceded my coming to that distinguished pulpit. Her home was a treasure house of beautiful things gathered from over the world. She was the denominational leader of women in missions, and her constant attendance upon the regular services of the parish was the assurance of peace in the mind of the pastor when he stood to preach. Her blending of a flawless sense of humor with gentle regard for another's confusion, and its perfect timing, is illustrated by what happened at the most embarrassing moment of my life.

It was an Easter morning. The church was crowded to capacity and the doors were closed. And it was then that I began the Lord's Prayer which followed the Invocation with "Now I lay me—!" I recovered to go directly into "Our Father Who Art in Heaven," but everyone in that vast congregation had heard. Until I die I shall remember my humiliation and horror. "If only I didn't have to open my eyes ever again," I thought. But presently I opened them to see the understanding and near hilarious smirks on the faces of that congregation.

At the close of the service Mrs. John Bussing came to me and said, "Dominie, you were so wonderful this morning and God must have made you do it! Always we shall have another picture of our dear pastor—at the knee of his mother."

Of course, there have been others who served as an added "means of grace." One I recall who came to me, looked appraisingly at my hair, and said, "I have always wondered how it stays so black." Well I knew that she had. I imagine that a Gremlin gave me a very unwise answer. "Why," I said, "I use my mother's dye." (Mother, at eighty-four, had practically no gray in her soft brown hair, though Father, at thirty, was almost white, and the children of our family are gray or not gray, accordingly.) The next Wednesday the Red Cross chapter was informed that "the Pastor dyes his hair, he told me so!"

The principal story within this story is the story of another woman. It is the story that binds all the elements together, the story of the one who has mothered my children and comforted and enriched my life. Through the years I have watched and experienced her faith and her way in prayer as they have grown to monumental proportions. Today, for her widely scattered children and for her more widely traveled husband, for her eyes that would have been blind had she not believed, for the agencies and programs she inspires, for tasks little and large, and for people—for so many people—she prays and has the answers. She demonstrates all the good that I would write and she has Peace with Power.

XVIII

Pray to Forgive

An enemy is a deadweight on your life—if you accept
the fact, or if you become his enemy. But so far as you
personally are concerned, you need have no enemy. Always prayer destroys an enemy, or in prayer you lose him.
Generally, too, the prayer that changes you changes him.
At any rate, I shall keep on praying, praying for him
or her, but chiefly praying for myself. Prayer not only
changes "things"; it changes people.

I read somewhere of a fond mother who was disappointed in her only daughter's choice of a husband; she
did not select the "right" son-in-law. It was irrevocable
and quite terrible. He just wouldn't do.

And then the disappointed mother-in-law got a bright
idea. She was a profoundly religious woman. She believed
in prayer and she decided to make the young husband
over! By prayer. Daily she prayed that he might become
the man she had hoped her daughter would marry, and

that prayer was answered. He became! Perhaps she became, too, but at any rate, that mother-in-law now has the finest son-in-law in the world. She admits it.

One Wednesday at noon I spoke at Schenectady at a pre-Easter service in a downtown theater. My subject was "reconciliation." As I spoke, two men came and stood directly in front of me. Oh, no, they were not really there, not in flesh and blood, and the audience could not see them, but for me they were there and they remained until I finished speaking. Then they went with me to my room. They were men who had been very close to me and from whom I was now estranged. As I sat in my room that afternoon, I went carefully through all the circumstances again.

Again I won the debate. I had been right. They were mistaken and wrong. That settled it. . . . Only it didn't. And presently I realized that winning the debate was definitely not a victory, for I had lost my friends. Being right in my own mind was not enough. I interrupted an important writing program that afternoon and all but missed a deadline the next day, but I got through to one of the most important decisions of my life.

I turned then from prayer to action. A telegram went to New York City and a letter went West. I said essentially the same thing in each; just about this, as I remember now: "I want things to be again as they were before. And before this Easter I come to you to ask forgiveness for anything that I have done, or anything you may think I have done that was not fair and right." That was about all. It was hard to think about doing, but when I actually came to doing it, it was *very* easy. And then? A reply telegram came from New York and presently a letter from the West. Each said essentially the same thing. That evening the telegram misted my eyes and broke my heart but to heal it. Like this it read: "No, Dan, I was wrong and I have been hungry for the old days. Let's get together very soon." We did, and it was almost as it had been before, but with something added.

One morning in another city, I opened the local paper to read that he had died the night before, that they had found him lying as though asleep, and then I was thankful and glad that I had sent the wire.

Not all the stories end like that, but I still pray, still follow that formula; and so *I* have no enemies and there is no breach.

When and where do I pray? At stated times? On my knees? In association with Bible readings and meditation? Yes, to each of these questions and to others you may think of asking. But there are no limits placed, and after all the questions are asked, there is still much beyond; for, you see, prayer is my life's breath, as it is or may be yours, and we breathe all the time.

Of course, at times we breathe harder, and at other times we stop to take a long breath.

I find myself mixing prayer with thoughts. I discover that when walking, especially when tramping in the deep woods, down quiet lanes, or across the high hills, or when I linger at a spring, the prayer of Communion keeps Him with me in full stride.

Dr. Norman Vincent Peale, my successor in the pulpit of the Marble Collegiate Church and my good friend, who is so inspiring, so wise a physician of souls, whose sermons and writings are a healing ministry to millions, once described that sometimes impatient interval when we wait for the green light as a rare opportunity to send and receive the flash of a prayer.

For five good years my ministry was associated intimately with the life of the greatest extemporaneous speaker of his generation, David James Burrell. On Sunday morning, while he still preached regularly, I would go from my study to his a few minutes before time to enter the pulpit, knock on his door, wait until I heard his resonant "Come in," and then enter and assist him with his robe. I had great delight in doing this.

One morning I forgot to wait—I just barged in. Dr. Burrell was kneeling by a chair set in a small recess, a chair in front of which he had dropped the red cushion, kneeling with his calendar for the day before him and with his face in his hands. Then I had his secret, or part of it.

Always he came back to his "Sacred Desk" from his knees. Always he found for himself and his waiting, expectant congregation Peace with Power in prayer.

He carried no manuscript and no notes into the pulpit, although his preparation was exhaustive; then on Monday morning he wrote or dictated the manuscript. But always, too, he wrote across a copy of the calendar for the day the rough outline of the sermon he was about to preach and carried that to the chair before which he knelt, burying his knees in the cushion, his face in his hands, and centering his faith in the One whom he loved, preached, and served.

That has been a good example for a younger man to follow.

Henry Ward Beecher, in one of the original Yale Lectures, the series now given his name, said, in effect, that great preaching is not out of books, but from the hearts and hungers of the people who come to hear. That is true of good and helpful preaching even when, by the Beecher standard, it may not be great. Preaching then to this formula and with the practices of David James Burrell, I have set the pattern of my pulpit career.

At the ordination of our second son, and our second to follow his father into the ministry, I told the story of the red cushion and then concluded with words which now seem almost prophetic, though certainly they were not so intended. Earlier I had spoken of three ways out of the ministry, and the third was "the way of triumph, the upward way, the way that is as the path of the just that shineth more and more unto the perfect day." Then I said in concluding my charge to the young man who sat facing us, with his eyes fixed upon his father, "It is this third way, the way of triumph, the shining path of the just, that holds my attentions tonight as I think of you, your ministry, and of its fulfillment. May you so preach and so minister through long and fruitful years, that when at last your earthly sun is set, no cloud shall float upon its sky. I do not ask for you freedom from hardship, exemption from sacrifice. I do pray that you shall have wisdom and power and good success." And again, though not perhaps as I had dreamed and hoped, but again, as always, prayer was answered. He came to Peace with Power.

In an Oregon valley stands a small white church that

once was the largest building in my small world. It was
built by my father, much of it with his own hands, as he
built other churches. But this white church bears now his
name and is a memorial to him and to the woman who
stood by his side, who very largely made him what he
became.

I watched that church rise from its foundation to its
variegated tower, stone on stone, board above board. I
played under its walls and later worshipped at its altar.
I sat in our family pew and would be happy were that
institution re-established throughout twentieth-century
America as it was known in those and earlier times.

There was good and even great preaching in that white
church, and music that was not ever bad; but there were
times when that modest sanctuary was filled by the voice
of one who had sung for the world outside and of another
younger voice destined to earn the wild applause of the
great cities of the East. There were commencement ex-
ercises in that church and lectures, for it was the chapel
of a "seminary" that began with some promise but that
presently moved away.

I remember all of these—the sermons, the music, the
commencements, the lectures, and the community occasions
that brought all together as perhaps only pioneer towns
ever meet. All of these were good, but best of all was the
prayer my mother prayed. There are ancient ones who
remember, too, after all these years, what a boy who was
there couldn't forget. She would talk about the "un-
searchable riches," this woman who was very poor of
riches. She would thank her God for "many things," and
her children wondered what they were, but now they

know. Her voice held the loveliest songs that ever came to that valley, but it was loveliest when she prayed. Always she prayed to the answer and always she found Peace with Power.

The preacher who built the white church, and who filled it then with the sermons of his faith, came back to it often for more than sixty years. I saw him last in that pulpit when he was nearly ninety. Then he smiled and listened to his sons. A few weeks later he had something to say and I think as I write that what he said then is the greatest sermon he ever preached. He was very tired and his voice had been very weak but now it was strong:

"I know that I am a dying man, but I am a victorious man. I have a message for the conference. Preach Christ, Preach Jesus Christ and Him crucified." He never spoke again. He didn't need to.

Prayer and Dr. Conwell

THE MAN who ever stands where Russell H. Conwell stood, stands where stood one of the greatest educators and religionists of his time. He was the pre-eminent lecturer in all American lyceum history. Also Conwell was a mystic. He saw things to come and he saw, or believed that he saw, beyond time and space and heard voices or received "landings" from beyond the grave. For more than a dozen years, in Philadelphia, I have stood where Conwell stood, in the pulpit of the church he founded and where, for nearly half a century, he conducted one of the most remarkable ministries in the history of the Protestant Church.

Baptist Temple became the largest and most widely known congregation of the denomination. In and with it he founded Temple University, which now has a dozen colleges, enrolls more than twenty-six thousand students, and is the largest of Pennsylvania's four state universities.

He created three hospitals, which have been united in the Temple University Medical Center. Dr. Conwell personally raised more than eleven million dollars for his various enterprises; some six million dollars from one lecture, which, in something more than fifty years he delivered more than six thousand times. This is recognized as the most famous lecture of the American platform, "Acres of Diamonds."

No man who knew Conwell, or who has studied his career, will deny that prayer was the heart of his message and the secret of his life's success. In everything, and about all concerns of his life, he talked to God as to his Omnipotent Friend. He was a genius in human understanding and in human relations; he had natural endowments in body and mind that were superlative; and though physically a veritable Hercules, he was as sympathetic and gentle as a woman. He was inter-faith and inter-race before there were organizations carrying the names, and he won marked success as a lawyer, a soldier, a newspaper man, and as servant of the State before, at thirty-seven, he became a preacher.

But his power was in prayer. Russell H. Conwell believed that the church, the hospitals, and the university were prayed into existence; that, again and again, they were saved from disaster by prayer, and that their amazing growth and enlargement was due directly to prayer.

Right here let it be written that Russell H. Conwell read the entire faith text! That text for him was always: "Now Faith is the substance of things hoped for and the evidence of things not seen. *But wilt thou know, O vain man, that faith without works is dead.*" Conwell's faith never went dead for lack of work on his part, and indeed from those who followed the brave flag he carried.

Sixteen hours out of every twenty-four was his work schedule, though more often he exceeded it. Eight hours for himself, he said, and eight hours for the lad Johnny Ring, who died serving him in the Civil War. It was this same Johnny Ring whose simple faith and unfailing prayers led Russell Conwell to Christ and into the Christian ministry.

Dr. William H. Parkinson, Dean of the Temple University Medical Center, who has led this institution to first rank among the world's medical schools, was one of Dr. Conwell's boys. He served with the great man when the battle to secure recognition for night education in the professions was being fought and won. Now, as no other living educator and administrator, he knows the story of Temple University. Dean Parkinson has told me of how in 1912 the trustees of the University, with funds exhausted, voted to close. But Dr. Conwell again prayed and got the answer.

The vote to close had been taken in Conwell's absence —on Sunday when he was at church! On Monday the trustees came to the great man's study and reported their action. They were received courteously and heard without comment. When they finished, Dr. Conwell said, in effect: "I am not surprised. I knew something like this was happening—must happen. I prayed all night. [Dr. Parkinson commented, "That meant *all* night."] Now I know that God has not brought us thus far to have us fail. Meet me here on Friday morning."

Between Monday and Friday the preacher-president

133

saw the Governor of Pennsylvania, Senator Penrose (with whom he was not too popular!), and, believe it or not, addressed a joint session of the state legislature in Harrisburg the day before it closed! Well, when any session of anything allowed Conwell to present his case, the case was won. That legislature voted 100,000 dollars to help the school for poor boys and girls, the school where, at minimum cost and at night, after a day's work, young people could study toward degrees in law, medicine, and practically all other professions. That vote and grant was the beginning of Temple University as a state university and the separation of the church and school.

On Friday morning the trustees came to Dr. Conwell's study again and heard how his all-night prayer had been answered.

In such manner he prayed for an organ. It is said that after a particularly intense period of prayer, bills were pushed under his door and checks came from people in faraway places—people unknown to the Doctor. Of course the world knew that Conwell was forever praying for something. When he died more than forty young men and women were still on his personal budget, receiving financial help from his lecture income.

As to the personal fortune of this man who earned millions, at his death his insurance had all been spent and his entire estate consisted of his home, which was the gift of the church. Speaking of the home, one of the present officers of Baptist Temple, who as a young man served under Conwell, once said, "It was a great relief to find that he hadn't gotten around to mortgaging it!"

Russell H. Conwell's only salary came from the church.

He remained as president of the College and University, as well as pastor of the church, until he died, but as president he never received a salary.

Dr. Conwell had a sense of humor, too. There are many stories about his fund of anecdotes and the way in which he could laugh at the failures when others saw only failure, and he went on to defeat them. One of the most characteristic of the stories involving his sense of humor has to do with the Bok award of 10,000 dollars given to the most distinguished Philadelphia citizen of the year, the man or woman who has made the greatest contribution to the public good, when such a one can be found. In the year the award went to Conwell—and it was the most popular ever made—a clergyman in the West wrote telling the Doctor he was building a church in a small, struggling community and that God, in a vision, had revealed to him that the 10,000 dollars was to be given to complete that church.

Dr. Conwell replied somewhat as follows: "Dear Brother, I am surprised at God. He knew that I gave that money away two years ago."

Russell H. Conwell preached his last sermon in his great church on Easter Sunday, 1925. Also he baptized a large class of men, women, and children. He was ill even then, and had been for months. He died of cancer on December 5 of the same year, after spending the entire night in his delirium presiding over a session of the University Board of Trustees.

Some would say that Conwell's last years particularly, though already I have written that he was a mystic, were clouded by his adventures into the occult. Others would say that as he came closer to the frontiers of the world and life beyond, the far-seeing eyes of his soul and his attentive ears saw and heard what he said they saw and heard. He believed that Mrs. Conwell came to him.

When so many were disturbed by his reports (and his always transparent honesty prompted him to speak) ; and when so many others ridiculed what he reported and grossly distorted or exaggerated what he said, he was grieved and became silent. Perhaps it was just as well, for those who do not have the seeing eyes and hearing ears— the unfortunate, insensitive ones—will always refuse to believe that such sight is ever given and such knowledge possible.

Dr. Conwell believed in physical healing by faith through prayer. He practiced his faith, prayed accordingly, and the years of his active life are crowded with the testimonies of those who were sure they had been healed. Here, again, the prayers of others were one with the prayer of a beloved pastor. When Conwell prayed, thousands who believed with him prayed with him, even as they worked with him. Together they did great things in the world—great things for men, women, and little children. The facts are on the record, and science has an explanation, but that explanation is not nearly enough.

Does my own ministry, which followed Conwell's, confirm in any particular his findings? Definitely, yes. Already I have written in this book of strength restored, sickness cured—of healing that came by faith through prayer.

As to seeing or hearing or receiving messages from "beyond," mine have been no more than intimations, with the constant growing sense of their presence. But my faith in

immortality does not stand upon these. I have never gone
to séances or their equivalent, never consulted mediums, or
associated with "sensitive" persons. I am satisfied with
what I have, and the words of Jesus in St. John's Gospel
have become increasingly of tremendous significance and
deep comfort to me.

I have read many books, and of these *The Unob-
structed Universe* by Stewart Edward White is easily the
best. But it has been my misfortune perhaps to see sad
and almost completely negative results from professional
activities in this field. The sorrowing have not been comforted and anguish has been exploited. Certainly I would
neither ignore nor belittle the search of sincere scientists
and specialists in this vast realm, but I would have those
who long to know and who wait expectantly for the sound
of a voice that is still go where I have gone to find what
I have found: "I will not leave you comfortless—I will
come to you" and "Ask and ye shall receive."

These are among the "intimations" that have come to
me directly, as similar intimations have come to many
others. They have been like pleasant whispers in the
friendly night.

When Mrs. Poling's sister died, she was vividly conscious into and with her last breath. I had promised to
tell her, and when the doctors gave me the word, I passed
it on to her. With that last breath, and immediately following it, for a perceptible, definite time, the girl's face
took on a radiance, a light that "never was on land or
sea." I saw it. Her father saw it. The men who loved
her and would have married her saw it. "She sees," they

said. Her face was filled, veritably crowded with surprise and glad recognition.

Twice I have dreamed of my mother, and the dream was more than a dream. Mrs. Poling too has dreamed the dreams that are definitely something more—even after Dr. Freud has told us "everything."

Twice I have had with me the presence of our son. Once riding in a compartment from London to Glasgow in February, 1943, when the word was still "Missing," not yet "Lost in Action." Then the "dream" was of such clarity that I heard the sea rush in and saw him, face to face. Long after that, under a bright sun, he was radiant with health and happiness. Then in altogether fitting association, I heard him speak. It was his voice—characteristically, completely his. He said, "Dad, you do love little children, don't you!"

There has been no other "dream" since that dream and I have not heard him speak.

Geoffrey O'Hara is one of America's famous composers. Perhaps his greatest song is "There Is No Death," the words of which were written by Gordon Johnstone. Many profoundly moving incidents are associated with this poem and the singing of its inspired words. In *Guideposts,* that unique little journal of faith and inspiration, some time ago Mr. O'Hara related the following:

"Years ago a concert singer came to me with a deeply moving story. A skeptic would have casually passed off the tale he told, but I listened intently. Music is a strong bond between people. Moreover, his story was about my song 'There Is No Death.'

"The tale he told concerned his mother. She had married an irresponsible man who immediately left her. After this marriage her father had disowned her, but when he discovered that she was destitute, he let her return—to live in a chicken coop, which he had made over, with a bed and scattered articles of furniture. In this chicken coop the singer-to-be was born. His mother died in childbirth.

"When the young boy grew up, he decided to take up singing as a career. Soon he acquired a fine reputation, toured the country, and always at the close of the program he would sing 'There Is No Death.'

"At this point the man's voice quickened with excitement as he gripped my arm tensely. 'Mr. O'Hara, just before I sing this song the most amazing thing always happens. My mother appears by my side. I can see her as well as I see you now. She smiles at me and places her soft hand on my shoulder. I feel it as surely as you feel my hand on your arm. She stands by my side until I finish the song. Then she is gone. . . .' "

Geoffrey O'Hara concluded: "I didn't mention that the words in the song affected me with the same electric effect, that shock waves coursed up and down my body when I wrote the music to these powerful words. This man's experience was similar to many others I have heard, all from people who had either lost their fear of death after listening to the song, or from those who had felt a similar contact with a departed loved one."

"I tell you they have not died,
   They live and breathe with you;
   They walk here at your side,
   They tell you things are true.

Why dream of poppied sod
When you can feel their breath,
When Flow'r and soul and God
Know there is no death.

"I tell you they have not died,
Their hands clasp yours and mine;
They are but glorified,
They have become divine.
They live! they know! they see!
They shout with every breath:
All is eternal life!
There is no death!"

In prayer I have found the reality of which Geoffrey O'Hara writes and the eternal truth of his great song. And this I know: "Because He lives, I shall live also."

XX

Prayer and Your Daily Task

M<small>Y MOTHER'S</small> open Bible in the chair behind the stove and the early morning prayer she whispered there were concerned directly for her life and work, which presently included her neighbors and the world, for she was like that.

"Father Moore," a farmer and one of my earliest and best friends, always prayed in the morning after he had read a chapter and always in his prayer was this sentence: "Help me to plow a straight furrow." That is a good prayer for any man.

It is well to pray for the strength and skill to do well your everyday tasks, never neglecting the words and thoughts of gratitude. The children of the house have a little prayer that, in spirit at least, and perhaps sometimes in words, should be remembered by their parents:

"We thank Thee for the bread we eat,
We thank Thee for the flowers so sweet,
We thank Thee for the birds that sing,
We thank Thee, God, for everything!"

In the Northampton Hospital following the family accident, I began a prayer from an ancient form that has become part of my regular morning and evening meditations: "I thank Thee, I praise Thee, I love Thee."

During all the nearly forty years of my Christian Endeavor and general youth activities and responsibilities, and indeed in all the other responsibilities I have carried, quite as definitely as in the work of church and pulpit, prayer has entered everything. And in this I have found myself companioned by my associates, with inspiring examples always on all sides of me—men and women of affairs to whom prayer was also their soul's breath and so appreciated.

The men and women of action in business and government and in responsible labor leadership, those who have shaped and directed grave matters in peace, as in war, and whom I have known intimately, have been and are men and women of constancy in prayer. There are now, as I have already written, groups of these executives and administrators meeting regularly throughout the nation, under the Capitol dome and over the world. Some of the most moving experiences of my life have been associated with those to whom I have gone in grave moments and trying ordeals of business depression or personal or family crises, and for whom and with whom I have prayed.

In a Christian Endeavor financial crisis, when without previous warning the International Headquarters Building was endangered and the organization was threatened with an overwhelming financial loss, executive officers and trustees prayed together; and directly there came the suggestion from one of the trustees that sent me to one who until that emergency visit I had not known. She answered our cry for help—more than answered it—and has become the greatest benefactor of the Christian Endeavor Society. With her money she has also given her humble and inspiring self and carried the message of the Movement around the world.

Christian Endeavor, with its millions of members in all churches of the Protestant faith, in all lands, and among all races, is a society brought into existence by prayer, and maintained and extended by the prayers of these millions. It is quite impossible to ledger the returns to the churches and to nations, to Christian unity, to brotherhood and good will, of this vast prayer investment of the young people of the world.

More recently the Christian Endeavor Executive Committee and the trustees voted to launch a nationwide "Mission to Youth," and quite outside of the budget, a considerable sum of money was required to finance the plan. Having resigned as President of the International or North American Society, while still continuing as President of the World's Union, I felt a very special responsibility for this particular campaign of my younger associates now carrying the heavier load.

I went to a city of the Middle West and talked to a

younger man who has followed his father in the adminis-
tration of one of the country's largest institutions in its
field. I have come to know as a man of prayer this man
who carries his religious profession into his business. Before I went to his office, I prayed in my hotel room, not
for money, but for the right decision. When I left my
room that day, I knew that possibly the answer would be
"No," but that I would get the *right* answer. The answer
was "Yes," but the amount of the underwriting asked
from this man, one-third of the total, was trebled before
we finished our conversation.

Christian Herald Association, as now organized, continues publication of the independent Protestant family
magazine founded by Louis Klopsch and T. De Witt Talmadge seventy-four years ago. This monthly journal, with
its 400,000 subscribers, and two million readers, is the
most widely circulated Protestant religious organ in the
world. In addition to publishing the journal, Christian
Herald Association owns and operates four great institutions in the broad field of human welfare. Mont Lawn,
the Children's Home at Nyack-on-Hudson, cares for boys
and girls of all faiths and races and is the first unsegre-
gated institution of its kind in the Metropolitan area. It
now maintains a year-round program. With its beautiful
permanent buildings and unique leadership, it is perhaps
the finest ministry of its kind in America.

The famous Bowery Mission, the first in its field, has
been for more than fifty years a Christian Herald enterprise. In the last fifteen years the physical property has
been enlarged, freed of debt, and the facilities and activities greatly expanded.

In China, Christian Herald maintains two orphanages and an industrial school in Foochow, the capital city of Fukien Province. The vicissitudes of famine and war have sadly interrupted this program, but within two years it has been strengthened by the forming of an intimate tie with "China's Children." Financial support for our program in China has greatly increased as the needs have grown.

In Florida the Memorial Home Community for retired religious workers and their wives is perhaps the most unique enterprise of its kind in the world. As the name implies, the Memorial Home Community is not an institution but a community, not of inmates but of residents. This memorial was erected in honor of his preacher father and mother, whose name it bears, by Mr. James Cash Penney, the distinguished Christian merchant. Within recent years, and with an initial endowment, he gave it to Christian Herald which now operates it along with these other activities. A million-dollar apartment building, with one and two-room furnished apartments, has been added, with quarters and clinical facilities and with a community doctor and nurse. Also, there are beautiful public rooms and a dining room.

Christian Herald's Family Book Shelf—"A Book Club you can trust"—is the latest enterprise. The success of this venture is clear-cut proof of the disgust of a large segment of the American reading public with current fiction and with reading clubs that exploit "pay dirt" in novels and stories.

Here is an institution and related activities that, with

the new mother building in central New York City, represent a total investment and property value of five million dollars. There is no debt, and in the past year there was an income from all sources of two million dollars. This was an increase in five years of 1,500,000 dollars.

This journal for all the family was, in the beginning, a creation of prayer, and today is a demonstration of the text "Ask and it shall be given you," and another vindication of the formula. "Faith without works is dead."

Again and again during the more than twenty years of my personal associations with these activities, the way ahead has been blocked and the final disaster seemed imminent when prayer and only prayer opened the road. Men were found who became God's agents in keeping these vast ministries alive, in saving them from failure, and in setting them at last on firm foundations where in their own integrity they pay their way and finance their constantly growing future of sevice to men, women, and children of all faiths, colors, and conditions. Faith has been the answer and prayer the way to success. Once a very great and wise man said in my hearing, "Prayer is worth millions of dollars—I have proved it. Prayer is the most practical thing in the world." Christian Herald has proved it too! Prayer has been "worth" literally millions of dollars to this association and certainly more than ten million dollars in these recent years of crises. If we consider the past, those great days before the Red Cross took over, when Klopsch and Talmadge and their successors were helping to feed and heal the plague-swept world, prayer, through this inspired journal, has found more than fifty million dollars to turn into food, medicine, clothing, literature, and shelter for those whom Jesus names "the least of these," who are especially the people of His love and care.

As to my own activities in these many and constantly enlarging affairs, this only I claim: prayer led me to those who have "done it"! If a man may worthily entertain pride, then my worthy pride is in those I have found and brought to many tasks, those with whom I have been and am associated—men and women of rare spirit, fine training, and very great ability. Younger than the writer, they have many years of service ahead of them; and were I now, even as I write, to lay down my editorial pen and cease from all my labors, Christian Herald Association, Christian Endeavor, and these other institutions would feel my loss (I hope!) only as the absence, the departure of a friend.

"Allied Youth," which in my opinion is the greatest youth adventure in the field of alcohol education and social action in our time, was the permanent result of the Campaign of Allied Forces. In the early 1930's, Allied Forces moved over the country in a national educational and speaking campaign in support of the Eighteenth Amendment and law enforcement. While I am honored with the title of Founder of Allied Youth and still continue to serve as a member of the Board of Trustees, others have been responsible for its constructive nonpolitical and unique youth program in the high schools and communities of the country. Allied Forces and Allied Youth were prayed into existence and "prayed through" to their success.

At the corner of Broad and Berks Streets in Philadelphia, in the heart of Temple University, is the Chapel of Four Chaplains. It is a memorial to the four *Dorchester* Chaplains, an interfaith shrine. It has three altars, one for each faith—Catholic, Jewish, and Protestant—and it will be open at all times to all people. Above the entrance burns an eternal light which calls all Americans to that unity which in life and death these four chaplains heroically demonstrated. It is not an argument or a debate, and in no sense a theological uniformity, but a symbol. This dedication is chiseled deep into the stone:

The Chapel of Four Chaplains, an Interfaith Shrine
Here is Sanctuary for Brotherhood
Let It Never be Violated

This Chapel, of which I am the first chaplain, was conceived in prayer, born in prayer, and through seven years of battle storm and post-war growing indifference, has moved, at times slowly, often through discouragement, but always through prayer, to success.

How could it have failed? Men, women, and children of all faiths prayed and worked together—even as the chaplains of the three faiths on the sea-washed deck of the sinking transport worked and prayed together until, having already given their life-jackets, they gave their lives and went down together.

This is the story of my faith. And in all the affairs, all the activities of my life, this story—whatever else it has been and however humble the things done—is the simple recital of one man's successful search through prayer to find Peace with Power.

XXI

Prayer and Peace

FOR ME the *Dorchester,* about which I have written in several preceding chapters, was another profound experience which helped solve the riddle of that amazing command of Jesus, "Love your enemies." It was in World War I that I first faced that command, and I realized that I could not fulfill it. I was terribly concerned about the matter and for a time it seemed that I must either become a pacifist to love my enemies or else renounce my Christian faith. On my knees I fought the problem through to a decision. But not until the *Dorchester* went down with her four chaplains did my intellectual and moral acceptance of the command "Love your enemies" become an actual experience within me. After that, I knew that I loved my enemies because the death of Jesus, the Son of God, for enemies and friends alike, has come alive for me in the death of my own son.

During the North African campaign of World War II,

I once attended a service prayer meeting held in an adobe hut of El Guetar, a village on the Gafsa front. A little group of GI's came through the blackout, sat on their helmets, and worshipped with their chaplain. That night the sergeant began the scripture reading with the first verse of the fifth chapter of St. Matthew's Gospel. When he came to the ninth verse, "Blessed are the peacemakers, for they shall be called the Children of God," he hesitated and then said, "I guess that's a good place to stop."

He and all those others who had his faith believed that they were peacemakers of their time. Every freedom they defended, every sacred value they protected with their lives, the very hope of winning the war—these they claimed not only for themselves and for us, but for all men everywhere, ally and foe alike. And the faith of those fighting men was realistic; for just as war cannot be isolated, peace cannot be. It must be universal and for all if it is to be at all. That to me is the meaning of the command "Love your enemies," in the will of God and after the manner of Jesus Christ.

I never signed a pacifist pledge. I was never a pacifist. In my student days I was an ardent disciple of Stanford's David Starr Jordan and in its field his *War and Waste* was my peace Bible. There I learned that war should not be and why. Also that a world war was no longer to be feared. I was taught that an armed conflict of world proportions could not be financed, and, anyhow, that international labor made such a war impossible—the worker would not fight the worker.

Then came World War I. I experienced a bit of it, caught a breath—just a breath—of its gas; watched men spitted on bayonets and scattered across a field; saw white skulls across a parapet. The Armistice followed, then Versailles, then Harding's "It must not happen again." We had won "the war to end war"—we had made the world "safe for democracy."

I was back in the pulpit now and New York and America were tuning in on prosperity. We had normalcy and a militant pacifism unequaled in history. It was the spring of 1921 and I sat with a group of leaders in a Manhattan luncheon club. One of these, distinguished in many fields, presented the first draft of a pacifist pledge presently signed by more than seven thousand clergymen and other religious workers. I was the only one present that day who could not and did not support the pledge. I said that without prejudice to any other man's conviction and certainly without judging any man, for me such a pledge was both unmoral and unchristian; that as a Christian I could not honestly pledge myself to a special behavior in advance of the particular event, the details of which could not be known. When reminded that I should have a Christian Absolute, I offered this: "God helping me, always I will be Christian."

Actually, aside from one man's conviction, it all seemed inconsequential since there would never be another war! But I continued to oppose the absolute or pacifist position and the circulating of its declaration, particularly among young people.

The futility of the specific pacifist pledge was presently demonstrated by the withdrawal of tens of thousands who signed such statements and by the fact that of four million signers of the so-called Oxford Oath in Britain, less than fifty thousand remained after the opening of World War II (the total number of conscientious objectors in England was less than fifty thousand). The tragedy of the pledge has confronted me around the world. Thousands of young people, persuaded by mature leaders whom they loved and trusted to take a position renounced in the face of later events, have become disillusioned and embittered.

In his *Newtopia,* P. W. Wilson writes: "People often remark that they cannot imagine Jesus bearing arms. But if there is to be what Thomas a Kempis called an 'imitation of Christ,' it must be a complete imitation, a reflection as in a mirror.

"Never in the annals of mankind has society called upon any man to bear arms who is comparable with Jesus. And why? Jesus never asked anything of society. Jesus had nowhere to lay His head and not one cent in His pocket. The whole of the life of Jesus was a service contributed to society.

"A conscientious objector who wishes to follow Jesus and receive the exemption from military service which was granted to Him without His ever having asked for it, has only to live as He lived, has only to be ready to die as He died. He must own no property that others than he have to defend. He must sleep under no roof that would be blown to bits if others did not chase away the raiders. He must sail in no ship that others at the risk of their lives have to convoy. He must marry no wife and father no children that others than he have to sustain and protect from the vicissitudes of war. He must devote his every hour of every day, as did Jesus, to helping others and must have no life that is outside the life in others. Let him fulfill these simple and obvious conditions and he will have little difficulty in sharing with Christ an exemption from military service."

Then as this preacher looks at war, does he disrespect or disregard the conscientious objector? Certainly not. For me pacifism would be both immoral and unchristian; but some of the finest Christians I know, men and women whose morals are above question, are pacifists. The draft law of the United States recognizes the status of the conscientious objector. Only in democratic Britain and America and in certain other democracies is this status granted, nor could democracy be democracy without such recognition. To say the least, it is a tragic waste when any citizen is destroyed or rendered useless because in conscience he cannot bear arms. There are so few of these and there are so many places where they may render vital service that, religious faith aside, not to recognize their status would be sheer waste. For the Church there is no worthy alternative but to companion her sons and daughters, comfort and guide them, wherever in conscience they go—to the colors or to the concentration camp or to service in a non-combat branch of war activity.

In one great state hospital for mental cases, eleven young men joined a dangerously depleted staff and, by doing the most menial work, rendered a vital social service. Receiving only two dollars and a half a month and their maintenance, living together in a cottage they kept clean, eating in the employees' cafeteria, and wearing the clothes issued to patients, they served their fellows and their country without violation of conscience. All were college men and some were qualified specialists in chemistry, architecture, and biology. The conscience of each would not permit him to serve where he might be called upon to kill or help kill his fellow beings. They did not take positions which might otherwise be filled by regular employees receiving salaries twenty times as large as their weekly allowances. They were only a part of a very considerable company recruited from conscientious objectors' camps.

No sharper distinction is made between the totalitarian states and the free nations than in their attitude toward the conscientious objector. In my own church, the register for conscientious objectors was established two years before Pearl Harbor. The first name on the register was that of a young man whose younger brother was one of the first of our congregation to enlist. This particular conscientious objector became a radio operator on a merchant ship on the North Atlantic and twice was on vessels sunk by enemy action. How can these things be! Well, I may have no answer for that question—but they are! Conscience must be inviolable if personality is to be sacred. Here is the heart of freedom. Both in civil law and in military regulations, our Government has recognized the right of the conscientious objector to be protected in his non-combatant beliefs. Certainly all law-abiding citizens should accept the logic of their Government.

But also the conscientious objector has an obligation to the Government which protects him. The right to hold particular beliefs and the privilege of trying to persuade others to accept them are not identical and they may be separated when circumstances warrant so doing. Trying to convert other citizens to becoming conscientious objectors in time of war, if successful on a large scale, would be interference with the armed forces of the nation at war. This is a recognized crime against the Government and a form of activity directly helpful to the enemy.

The pacifist should face the fact that recognition of his status enjoins upon him within that status the same acceptance and obedience required of the soldier. When, for instance, he refuses to register, if required to do so in the status recognized, he may still claim the right of his conscience, but he has forfeited his legal right to any further consideration and should, as he generally does, go to jail just as the soldier for comparable legal delinquency goes to the guard-house or before a court martial. Not to register, or to incite others not to, is clearly civil disobedience or, otherwise stated, anarchy.

During the war I received a letter from one of my friends who is a pacifist. He is grateful to America for the recognition of the status of the conscientious objector and, on his part, appreciates the difference between the dictatorships and the democracies. What this man has to say should be read by all who stand with him. "If my absolute position," he has written, "keeps me not only out of the army, but out of all service associated with the military, then without seeking special consideration or crying for help, I should pay the price, go to prison, or suffer whatever is required, exactly as the soldier pays the price, offers his life for what he believes to be his duty."

That is in contrast to a statement made by another citizen who, immediately following the attack on Pearl Harbor, spoke out vigorously in public against Japanese treachery. He said that he would not bear arms, but that he was offering his services to the civilian defense; that he would be willing and eager to take the most dangerous assignments, even to join the squad digging out delayed bombs. Such a public declaration, however fine the individual's spirit, is inimical to free government. Is it not a presumptuous thing? If in a national crisis every man were in public announcement to tell his Government where he would and would not serve, then we would have not a defense but a debacle.

The Government recognizes the status of the conscientious objector, but the Government does not and cannot grant to the conscientious objector or to any other man the right to choose in the manner described.

The pacifist is responsible for being honest with his fellow Christian who is not a pacifist. A Protestant missionary journal, in September, 1941, supported a quoted statement that this was just another war of imperialistic powers to see who would shove whom around! The same journal, in March, 1942, published an editorial under the caption, "Japanese Fiendishness and Nazi Brutality Compared with American Barbarism." No Christian would question the indictment of the lynching incident described in the editorial as barbarism. I would use even more violent language. But in this instance the connotation did not strengthen America in her struggle to survive and did give comfort to the dictators. Surely this is not pacifism; indirectly it was support for Nazi Germany, Fascist Italy, and military Japan.

In an article written by a distinguished clergyman are these words: "I found that my President and Congress and everybody else who said that murder and slaughter and lying and sinning would bring peace and prosperity and a united world were wrong—hideously wrong. Apparently they forgot what kind of world this is and that you can't sow evil and get good, you can't fulfill the conditions of hell and get any semblance of Heaven." Well, of course, the President and Congress never said it, nor did they believe it. This is rhetoric, but also it is untruth. Neither do I believe that we can sow evil and get good, nor do I preach that a righteous peace, Christ's peace, will come directly out of an unholy war. But a righteous peace, Christ's peace, must come *after* war or it will never come at all.

The man who said "It does not make any difference who wins the war, if God loses it" was offering a credo of defeatism.

At the opening of World War II a minister of unquestioned sincerity came to me with the following statement: "The son of my senior elder has just been called up. He is a youth leader in my church. He has followed me closely and with confidence in my moral leadership. Ten days ago he came and said: 'I have no moral alternative but to go to the colors. The theory fades before the fact. My conscience will not allow me to claim exemption—but that is not all. . . . Pastor, if what you have said concerning war is true and *if now you have nothing further to say,* then in going to the colors I leave my church, I leave my God—I go to hell!' "

Not every preacher faced it like that, but not every draftee was as frank and as analytical as was this preacher's young friend. To such a man, what is to be said?

First, let it be said that Christian faith must not be rationalized, for then it would be neither Christian nor a faith. But for a vast majority of all Christians, faith and life must be reconciled. Only a small minority choose the monastery and live apart from life. This reconciliation is not for yesterday but for today. Life is no longer a debate, it is a practice; no longer a theory but a fact. No man may choose for another. Christianity makes choice imperative, but individual and free. "Whatsoever He saith unto thee, do it" is the high command of the Christian's soul. But the experience of one Christian may be shared with another and may even become a safe guide for another.

I accept, for my family and property, police protection. I want more of it rather than less. I claim it in spite of the fact that I know the officer of the law in the line of duty may take a life or lose his own. The fact that I do not have actual physical responsibility for the deed of the officer does not relieve me of moral responsibility; and surely, for the Christian, moral responsibility at least equals physical responsibility. As a member of the community, I have moral responsibility for every life lost in the use of police force, nor could I excuse myself from such responsibility by insisting that I do not ask for or desire police protection.

It is here that Tolstoi posed the absolute. He concluded that he would not use, nor would he sanction, force— even to protect the person or life of his mother; that were she to suffer physical attack, he would be compelled to remain inactive in the presence of the act. But by such refusal, he would still have moral responsibility for the unrestrained act. I would rather assume physical responsibility for slaying the murderer than accept moral responsibility for the murderer's crime.

There is no escape. Each of us is a social unit. Choice may affect the particulars but cannot change the principle.

If I accept and support police protection for the community, then as a Christian and a citizen I am bound to support the principle when it is lifted to cover the immeasurably greater values of a nation. And if I accept the principle for the nation, then in simple logic and as a Christian I cannot escape supporting the principle when it is lifted to cover human freedom in all the world. Practically, neither war nor peace can be isolated. Presently, no nation can possess freedom unless all may have it.

A young ministerial student who enlisted in the Marines and went to San Diego in January, 1942, had a roommate who was a conscientious objector and who at about the same time went to a camp for objectors. There was no misunderstanding between the two friends. Each appraised and valued the decision of the other. But the young Marine wrote to his friend as follows: "There is no escape for either of us. We are both in. You follow your conscience to camp and support the Government as in good faith you may. And by that support, by your very citizenship, you help maintain the military establishment. I have the gun on my shoulder and you help keep it there."

I cannot escape the logic of the young Marine. Your son and mine are at the controls, or on the fighting deck, or in the ranks. They are there and we are here, but we are feeding shells into their cannon, gas into their tanks, and we, with them, are morally bound to the physical event. There is just one way, and only one way, for any man to stay out of war—*keep war out of the world*.

The absolute position of Tolstoi would seem to relieve the situation, and some there are who in conscience cannot plow a field, bear a stretcher, or pay taxes to a government at war. But these do not escape responsibility for inaction in the presence of the fact. Also they participate, participate by compelling the community to feed and care for them, while it, in equally good conscience, struggles to maintain its very existence.

A distinguished London clergyman, a leader of British pacifists, awoke one day to discover that his support of the League of Nations' Sanctions against Italy during the Abyssinian incident, his very sermons and prayers for peace, had become support of war, for Italy declared that if the oil sanctions were imposed she would fight. He could refuse to go to war and would be bound so to do. But he could not escape his share of responsibility for the creation of an international incident in which other men would fight and die.

Now, to the Christian rises the question: "In such a circumstance, what would Jesus do?" There were occasions when Jesus, the tender and compassionate Saviour, the healing Great Physician, became the master of flaming anger. Perfectly He distinguished between evil and the evildoer, and hate for any person was never in His heart. But He was the angry Christ where anger was the imperative. Then He was the "Terrible Meek." Even so, I have never found Him behind a bayonet, nor did I ever know a man in the service who wished Him there. We wanted Him not in that business, though to Him we turned for grace to see the business through. No, the question is not "What would Jesus do?" but "What would Jesus have me do?"

Does one say, "Surely Jesus would not have a follower do what He, Himself, would not do?" For some of us, certainly He would! Would Jesus have a surgeon do in a case of cataract of the eye what the New Testament states He did? Would he have twentieth-century scientists mix mud with spittle and anoint cataract-blinded eyes? Surely, not that. The surgeon has limitations that Jesus did not have. Also, he has instruments, medicines, and laboratory knowledge that were not available when Jesus operated in Galilee. Jesus does not expect me to do what He did. He would not expect me to feed five thousand people as He fed them, but He does expect me to do what I can and may toward feeding the hungry.

"Love your enemies; do good to them which hate you." Does Jesus Christ mean that for today? Definitely, yes!

In a letter written by a young graduate student in the University of West Virginia are these words: "This love is not the soft thing that we have thought. It is different. It is hard. It is sacrificial. It dies, and may even become responsible for bringing physical death—but it does not shirk duty nor does it fail."

Would we do good to those who hate us if without resistance we surrendered freedom, or if we consented to the destruction of democracy, or if we allowed that which is infinitely more precious than physical existence to be destroyed while we remained alive and untouched? Realistically, would we love those who are now, in the military sense at least, our enemies or potential foes if we gave the world order of the dictators an unhindered entrance into the lives of unborn generations? Ours is a world grown small. Oceans no longer divide—they unite. The Scripture is fulfilled; we are "one of another," and here we have no choice. But it is for us to choose whether we shall be hopefully or hopelessly one of another.

This, too, is the realism of "Love your enemies." It is not yet Christian perfection but it is humanity struggling to survive. It is that most sacred thing, personality, battling to win over the twentieth-century deluge of the absolute state. It is the Christian rising to choose defense of freedom as the alternative to slavery, and lifting his eyes from the red hands of his bloody business—lifting them, it may be, to the cross of redemption and crying for forgiveness. It is Abraham Lincoln's "With malice toward none, with charity for all," . . . "we strive on to finish the work we are in."

One of the most moving documents coming out of World War II is a letter written by a Dutch lad to his father just before he and his three companions were shot to death by a German firing squad. The letter concluded: "We are courageous. Be the same. They can only take our bodies. Our souls are in God's hands. That should be sufficient consolation. I am going—until we meet again in a reunion which will be so much happier. May God bless you all. Have no hate. I die without hatred. God rules everything."

And there is something more. In this realism is the *strength* that justifies both a dynamic patience and an unfaltering faith that the next war shall be stopped before it starts.

This then is the incomplete statement of my philosophy with regard to war and peace.

Whatever else may be said about it, this I know: I came to it through long study, continuing prayer, and in what was, at times, a veritable agony of love. But at the end there was, for the assigned tasks that took me over the world in World War II, Peace with Power. In those days, for myself and others, I claimed and found that always *"His grace is sufficient."*

XXII

Prayer and My War Missions

Beginning in July, 1941, when I was summoned to Washington, D. C., and found myself, within twenty-four hours, flying in a B-24 to London, the next five years, the war years, and the succeeding three years, found me spending from two to seven months of each year in special missions associated with the nation's war effort. On all these missions I traveled with letters from the President of the United States and the Chief of Chaplains of the Army. On one mission I carried credentials from the Chief of Staff. Frequently I represented the churches of my faith through the Federal Council of the Churches of Christ in America, or the World's Christian Endeavor Union, and always I was a war correspondent, being accredited to the *Philadelphia Record,* the *Christian Her-*

FAITH IS POWER—FOR YOU

ald, or with assignments from *Time,* the *Philadelphia Enquirer,* and the *Christian Science Monitor.**

My missions took me fourteen times across the Atlantic by air and four times across the Pacific. I visited every active theater of the war and all postwar occupied areas, traveling more than 200,000 miles in these journeys. These matters are not written here as biographical, but to give the setting for and to suggest the intense circumstances under which my daily prayer life grew to meet the imperative requirements of mounting physical, mental, and spiritual needs.

That first mission to London came in the months immediately preceding Pearl Harbor and at the telephoned request of Ambassador John Winant whom I had come to know intimately and who believed that I could be helpful in certain matters that involved a lack of understanding on the part of British churches of America's attitude toward the war effort of the "Allies." London was just then staggering up from the appalling hurts of the Blitz. During that visit I met with churchmen and with congregations of all the faiths and saw the leaders of the war effort. Among these were Prime Minister Winston Churchill; Foreign Secretary Anthony Eden; the Archbishop of Canterbury; the Cardinal of the Roman Catholic Church; the President of the Free Church Council;

**Publisher's Note:*

Dr. Poling was the first clergyman to receive the Medal for Merit (dated March 29, 1947), highest civilian award given by this country. He was also awarded the War Department Citation for "outstanding and conspicuous service as a war correspondent. . . ." *See* Appendix.

and the executive committees of the British Christian Endeavor Union and of other youth organizations.

I flew over by way of Gander, in Newfoundland, then just beginning to assume importance as the port destined to become to the Allies the most vital in the North Atlantic area. We reached London by way of Lisbon, Portugal, Dublin, Ireland, and Prestwick, Scotland. I returned Pan American by way of Ireland, Portugal, the Azores, and Bermuda. While the particulars of travel are not the vital matter, they involved flying in every type of commercial and military plane, and down every route of flight across Africa, East and West and North and South; across all the oceans, continents, and all the major islands. Once we flew the "Hump" into China, following the valleys to avoid enemy ships; and once at an altitude of 23,000 feet for the same reason.

In the Pacific I spent an unforgettable period with the senior chaplains of the Army and Navy, Colonel Ivan L. Bennett and Captain Reuben Schrum, visiting the island bases throughout the South Pacific. Preceding and following this mission, I was the guest of Australia as the Turnball Foundation Preacher and good-will messenger in historic Scots Church, Melbourne.

Following the close of actual conflict, I was asked to continue my overseas activities; and again, with the cooperation of all the services, I traveled three times to Europe—England, France, Italy, and Germany. In the spring of 1949, on invitation of General Douglas MacArthur and the senior chaplain in the Far East, Chaplain (Col.) Roy L. Parker, I went to Tokyo to participate in the Easter services there. In connection with this mission, as a member of the President's Committee on Religion and Welfare in the Armed Services, I visited the bases throughout the Pacific—Hawaii, Johnson Island, Kwajalein, Guam, Japan, Korea, the Philippines, Okinawa, China, the Aleutian Islands, and Alaska. In the summer of 1949, the President of the United States appointed Chaplain Parker Chief of Chaplains of the Army, with the rank of Major General. This appointment was a merited honor to a man of many service distinctions in his high calling, which, in years before the war and during it, took him over the world and to every front of conflict. I had been with him in the United Kingdom, in Algeria, Tunisia, at Headquarters in Washington, and finally in the Far East before he returned as Chief.

One night on Bougainville in the Pacific, I was called out of my rollup to meet a chaplain who was accompanied by a lad from my own congregation in Philadelphia. We had just arrived, flying in on a C-47 with one engine and after skirting positions still held by the enemy. Fighting was still intense on Bougainville then. Our tent opened toward the glow that lighted the volcano which was eleven miles away, and in the morning the boy who came to me that night was going back to the line under the volcano. He wanted to be baptized. He had just missed baptism at home. His draft number came up and he was hurried away. That night we made the arrangements, and very early the next morning, before he started back to that lonely, desperate jungle front, Howard March came with his chaplain. We went a little way into the jungle, sat on a palm log, and I instructed him, received his confession, and knelt with him in prayer.

We came back then to the hastily-improvised jungle chapel—a tarpaulin thrown over a palm log, jungle flowers in shall casings on an altar made from orange crates. Assisted by the chaplain, I baptized the young man and sent him forward with my prayers. He said that he was ready now to go, ready as he had never been before.

You may be sure that later, when word reached me that Howard March had been killed in action, I was glad that I had been there not only to baptize him and to pray with him, but to receive him into his mother's church.

This story has an unusual, happy ending, for one Sunday morning some time later, Howard March came down the aisle in Philadelphia to convince me that the announcement of his death had been a mistake! He had been wounded, but had made a good recovery.

To me, that first mission to England in 1941 is forever memorable because of its association with John Winant. John Winant, who, of all the men in public life I have met and known, was the most selfless. He was a profoundly religious man and among his closest friends were religious leaders both in the United States and abroad. Dr. Temple, Archbishop of Canterbury, whom Mr. Winant greatly admired, became my friend through the Ambassador.

When I landed in London one Sunday evening, just in time to escape the blackout, I found a note awaiting me at the Embassy. The Ambassador had been called suddenly to a conference and would meet me in my hotel room at seven o'clock in the morning. When we met in the morning, I learned that he had dined the night before at Buckingham Palace with the King, Churchill, and Eden. We spent two hours then in considering together how my

171

visit and time could be used to the best advantage. After that first morning, there were other times, but never another quite like that.

As he sat relaxed on the couch, with his long legs crossed, I saw that there was a large hole in his shoe. He grinned when he noted the direction of my eyes, showed me the hole in the other shoe, and said, "The King has a hole in his, too!" Leather was a scarce commodity in London then. Conditions became much better for us, at least, after Pearl Harbor and with the arrival of our Army supplies.

Once John Winant went with me to a meeting of clergymen of the Free Churches. The great Baptist statesman Dr. John Rushbrooke presided. I introduced the Ambassador. Always he spoke with deliberation—indeed, there were times when he was painfully deliberate, with pain that was felt by everyone present who suffered for him! And yet he was one of the most genuinely eloquent men to whom I have listened. That day he was deliberate, to say the least. He seemed shy and embarrassed, but presently he became alert and vocal and what he said was like a sermon from a pulpit or a benediction before an altar. I have not seen it anywhere in print, but I am sure he must have used it before; it was of such a poignant quality, so perfect and even classical, as well as profoundly spiritual. The words spoken there could be his own worthy epitaph: "You (the English) have said so little. You have done so much. It is all part of a soldier's faith—to have known great things and to be content with silence."

As we drove back to the Embassy that afternoon, I reminded him of what he had said and told him how greatly I regarded it. He was silent for what seemed a long time and then he replied, "Dan, I do not know how men live at all, how they can survive, without faith, faith in God, a faith that lives in them—whatever!" And his last tragic illness made that confession of his faith all the more significant. Faith that is adequate—"Whatever!"

And so I traveled on. Everywhere, among the humble and the great, I found my prayer life drained to its depths and my faith again and again tested until I fairly wept in my fear of losing it altogether. But that fear was never more than a passing mood, self-confessed in some lonely moment, but never voiced and soon—very soon—gone from me as I saw faith marching, suffering, and dying.

Always my cry was heard. Always when I "asked," I was answered. Always for myself and for those to whom I came under every circumstance of fear and of pain which tore the body and racked the mind, His grace was sufficient. He and His peace never failed. Often all else did.

For the ordeals of war, as it had been before the war and as it continues to be, prayer was and is the road to Peace with Power.

173

XXIII

Palm Sunday, 1943

I WAS SITTING in a bucket seat of a C-46, of all the ships
the one least desired by men and crews—at least when
they first came into general service during World War
II. It was Palm Sunday, April 19, 1943, and we were
flying north to Miami from Natal, the great base in Brazil, flying back from Tunisia and Algiers. We had spent
a night en route on Ascension Island, that dot in the
South Atlantic below the Equator where American engi-
neers tore a mountain apart to make a runway long
enough for the C-54's. Engine trouble made our unsched-
uled delay necessary.

Palm Sunday . . . and now above islands in the Caribbean I was reading in my New Testament, reading
again the story of Christ's triumphal entry into Jerusalem.
". . . on that day much people that were come to the
feast—when they heard that Jesus was coming to Jerusalem, took branches of palm trees and went forth to

meet him and cried, 'Hosanna, Hosanna, Blessed is the King of Israel, that cometh in the name of the Lord.' "

I became conscious of someone standing in front of me and, looking up, saw that it was Robert Sherwood, author and playwright. We met on a crossing back in 1941 when I was returning from London from my first mission, and he, beginning his activities in one of the most important civilian assignments of the war, was on his way from the American Embassy in London to the White House. Then delayed for five days by weather in the Azores, we saw a good deal of each other and became well-acquainted.

On that earlier flight, in September, 1941, via Pan American, we did not sit on bucket seats, but on the "plush" (and there *is* a difference!), for that flight was not in wartime. Then I had other distinguished traveling companions, among them Lord and Lady Halifax returning to their post in Washington, D. C., after a short vacation at home in England. Lord Halifax, sitting quietly in his section, spent nearly all of his time with his Bible and Prayer Book.

Now, above the Caribbean, Robert Sherwood, steadying himself, bent his rugged six feet seven and handed me a Testament from which he had been reading. It was opened at the flyleaf, on which was a personal message from Sherwood's intimate friend, the President, beginning: "Dear Bob . . ." That message commended the little book as one that was an inspiration and guide to the giver, who believed that it would also be that to Robert Sherwood on his journeys.

One of the servicemen moved over and Sherwood sat

down. We talked then into Miami, and that was not too long, for whatever else was said about and against the new C-46, she was not a loiterer. We talked about the "duration" and agreed that things had begun to brighten. But chiefly we talked about the rumor that Russia was going to make a separate peace with Germany, and an even more frightening rumor that Hitler had the Bomb. Now we are inclined to forget the rumors and uncertainties that were so real in late 1943 when we condemn some of the actions taken by Churchill and Roosevelt to hold Russia as our ally.

But before and after we discussed the war situation and what we were leaving behind in North Africa, we talked of Palm Sunday—to me the most significant Palm Sunday of the many I had celebrated, perhaps the most significant of all I shall celebrate. It was the first since the *Dorchester* went down and only seventy-six days after that fated sinking. Also I knew then that Clark's wife, Betty, was in the hospital awaiting their second child. When I reached Miami a telephone call brought the welcome word that the little daughter, Susan Elizabeth, named after two grandmothers and her mother, had arrived with safety for both mother and child.

The New Testament in Robert Sherwood's hand was an introduction to a discussion of the religious life and practices of the wartime President of the United States. The country knew that he came of a long line of Episcopalians and earlier Dutch forebears, and that he himself was a warden in the family church at Hyde Park. But generally the deep religious life of the President was not known, for it was not worn casually or ostentatiously on his outside coat. As Robert Sherwood said that day—or was it at another time later—"He is both liturgically and personally a deeply religious man." And by "personally" he made very clear the fact that he did not mean in any public or shallow fashion, but in the manner of his message written on the leaf of the copy of the New Testament Scriptures given to his friend. Religion was one of the "two things" Robert Sherwood said President Roosevelt did not discuss.

Some time in late 1944 I wrote the President asking him whether he might wish to write a special Easter message for *Christian Herald,* a message on immortality. My request was presumptuous and I knew it. But quite apart from the natural desire of an editor to score a "scoop," I knew that should he write such a message, it would comfort and reassure many people.

Weeks passed and I had given up hope—or had I? The fact that I had received no courteous secretarial note from my good friend William Hassett, telling me that I should have "known better," did keep hope alive. And then, just in time to meet the "deadline" for the Easter issue, the message came—and what a message it was! Perhaps no other word of a President, or of any other comparable public official anywhere, has ever approached that simple, brief, but comprehensive and poignant declaration of personal faith in immortality. The President's statement was read after he had gone on to know its reality. I am glad that I had the opportunity to thank him for it personally. It reads:

"Here in Washington, and across the Potomac in Virginia, we see many noble monuments to the glorious dead —to the Americans whose souls go marching on. But these monuments would be meaningless did they not symbolize something very profound within all of us and that is, faith in the eternally living spirit.

"That faith becomes all the more powerful in these tragic days of war. Out of suffering comes a renewal of the life of the spirit. Then men who have gallantly given their lives have turned our thought to religion—to a realization of man's dependence upon the Providence of God.

"The story of the Resurrection is the expression of man's highest aspiration; it is the story of man's greatest victory—his triumph over death; it is a source of consolation for those whose loved ones have given their lives and a source of inspiration for all generations yet unborn."

There is a sequel to the story of this Easter message. One morning Robert Sherwood was called into the President's office and handed my letter requesting it. The President said, "Bob, I want to do this for Dr. Poling," and then he began to talk while Sherwood took notes— this was his method.

When the President had finished, Sherwood went into the old Cabinet Room, organized his notes, and typed them. Returning to the President, he handed the rough manuscript to Mr. Roosevelt, who thanked him but did not discuss the matter further, and Robert Sherwood never saw the statement again until, as the President had revised it, it appeared in *Christian Herald*.

On the night the President died, Mr. Sherwood read his friend's profoundly moving declaration of faith over a world network.

I had known the President rather well when he was the Governor of New York, but he came to the Presidency under conditions that put me, with such strength and influence as I had, in "the opposite corner"—and where, were that campaign to happen again, I would be again!

I had continued my opposition, but the war obliterated partisanship; and so when one afternoon the White House asked me to respond to Ambassador Winant's request and go to London, I started the next morning.

For the next four years I served under the President, whom I came to regard with deep affection. We never discussed the other matters—they were left for the Peace he never saw. But as I went over the world, I found President Roosevelt, as no other man in the rocking world of the Allies, loved and trusted by the "little people." He was the symbol of their hopes and aspirations, and no other name was comparable to his.

Once I visited a Berber village in the Atlas Mountains, remote from civilization and out of touch save only as the French authorities collected the tax. The Headman was most cordial to the visiting Americans. His community was small and very poor, one of the groups of this strange, non-Arab white race whose origin is shrouded in mystery. They number perhaps 250,000 men, women, and children and inhabit the high mountains in North

Africa. They are Mohammedans, but hold themselves severely apart. Their women never veil and they are scrupulously honest.

The Headman who received us lived in a typical Arab black tent and cave. The tent was the entrance to the cave, which was natural, but had been enlarged. There were many goatskins on the dirt and stone floor, but save for cooking utensils, no other furnishings. One thing caught my eye—a picture on the pole of the tent. The only object above the level of the floor, it was the cover, in color, of a French pictorial printed in Algiers. It was the picture of President Roosevelt.

I have ten personal letters written by the war President during the five war years of his life, and one cablegram. The letter that is, I think, the most revealing, is the shortest of the ten, dated November 13, 1944. I quote the second and concluding paragraph:

"Dear Dr. Poling:

". . . I hope I shall prove equal to the solution of the problem which you put so succinctly and with such force in your statement to the *Daily Record*. In these grave days I like to think that I shall continue to have a remembrance in your prayers.

Very sincerely yours,
(signed) Franklin D. Roosevelt"

I saw the President only once after receiving that letter—nine days before he went for the last time to Hot Springs, Georgia. I had been in the White House offices on business that did not require an interview with him, and I was leaving through the front reception room when

I was called back. I was told that the President wished to see me.

When I came into the great room, he was seated at his desk and smiling. Characteristically he pushed back from his desk with his left hand and threw up his great head. There was nothing of importance and I was with him not more than five minutes. He looked much better than at any time within the year—his face had even a little color, I thought, and his voice was stronger. Certainly I was reassured as to his physical condition.

Always I shall remember his last words to me. They were the words I heard from the lips of a dying boy in an Army hospital in France. President Roosevelt threw up his right hand and said:

"I'll be seeing you!"

XXIV

Prayer and Miracles

Every faith and all religions "believe" in miracles and have the equivalent of "Lourdes." Even scientists have recorded and seriously regarded happenings for which there were no satisfactory explanations. They seemed, at least, to be quite beyond the operation of any natural law.

To the believing Christian the "miracle" is never either against or beyond law, though it may be quite beyond man's understanding of law. But God is also a God of law and not limited now or ever by man's knowledge or lack of knowledge of law.

Dr. Arthur Compton, the distinguished physicist and Nobel Prize winner, who is a Christian, has written in effect that perhaps God's direct intervention in human affairs ceased some five or six thousand years ago when man might reasonably be judged to have achieved moral and intellectual stature justifying the confidence that he could now assume full responsibility for his affairs. Recent events may have shaken that confidence! However, God thinks in eons and sees beyond them, while we live and die in our own generations.

Already I have included the miracle in this story of my personal faith. I would add now other supporting material. In March, 1941, the *Reader's Digest* printed a remarkable confession of faith written by Alexis Carrel, M.D., of the Rockefeller Laboratories, one of the world's most distinguished scientists. Previously I have quoted briefly from this article. I came to know Dr. Carrel, and I talked with him about these and other associated matters included in his widely circulated book *"Man, the Unknown."*

Dr. Carrel wrote of prayer only indirectly, but inclusively of the miracle. Prayer was also his way, not only to the miracle, but to Peace with Power.

When I saw Dr. Carrel the last time, he said that he was interested now in man's immortal spirit. He referred to one of the last statements of Charles Steinmetz, who said that the great discoveries of the future would be in the realm of the spirit, and then Dr. Carrel concluded in a veritable rapture by declaring that if he could find eleven men as selfless as those who followed Jesus, he, with them, could accomplish now a revolution in human affairs as vast as that which was wrought by the disciples, their contemporaries, and successors.

The distinguished scientist's article first published in the *Reader's Digest* was later printed in the *Congressional Record* of the Second Session of the Eightieth Congress.

It so closely reflects my own experience that I share a considerable portion of it with the readers of this book:

"Prayer is not only worship, it is also an invisible emanation of man's worshipping spirit—the most powerful form of energy that one can generate. The influence of prayer on the human mind and body is as demonstrable as that of secreting glands. Its results can be measured in terms of increased physical buoyancy, greater intellectual vigor, moral stamina, and a deeper understanding of the realities underlying human relationships.

"If you make a habit of sincere prayer, your life will be very noticeably and profoundly altered. Prayer stamps with its indelible mark our actions and demeanor. A tranquility of bearing, a facial and bodily response are observed in those whose inner lives are thus enriched. Within the depths of consciousness a flame kindles. And man sees himself. He discovers his selfishness, his silly pride, his fears, his greeds, his blunders. He develops a sense of moral obligation, intellectual humility. Thus begins a journey of the soul toward the realm of grace.

"Prayer is a force as real as terrestrial gravity. As a physician I have seen men, after all other therapy had failed, lifted out of disease and melancholy by the serene effort of prayer. It is the only power in the world that seems to overcome the so-called laws of nature; the occasions on which prayer has dramatically done this have been termed miracles. But a constant, quieter miracle takes place hourly in the hearts of men and women who have discovered that prayer supplies them with a steady flow of sustaining power in their daily lives.

What Prayer Is Not

"Too many people regard prayer as a formalized rout-ine of words, a refuge for weaklings, or a childish petition for material things. We sadly undervalue prayer when we conceive it in these terms, just as we should under-estimate rain by describing it as something that fills the bird bath in our garden. Properly understood, prayer is a mature activity indispensable to the fullest development of personality—the ultimate integration of man's highest faculties. Only in prayer do we achieve that complete and harmonious assembly of body, mind, and spirit which gives the frail human reed its unshakable strength.

"The words, 'Ask and it shall be given to you,' have been verified by the experience of humanity. True, prayer may not restore the dead child to life or bring relief from physical pain. But prayer, like radium, is a source of luminous, self-generating energy.

Strength Through Prayer

"How does prayer fortify us with so much dynamic power? To answer this question (admittedly outside the jurisdiction of science) I must point out that all prayers have one thing in common. The triumphant hosannas of a great oratorio, or the humble supplication of an Iro-quois hunter begging for luck in the chase, demonstrate the same truth: That human beings seek to augment their finite energy by addressing themselves to the infinite source of all energy. When we pray we link ourselves with the inexhaustible motive power that spins the universe. We ask that a part of this power be apportioned to our needs.

186

Even in asking, our human deficiencies are filled and we arise strengthened and repaired.

"But we must never summon God merely for the gratification of our whims. We derive most power from prayer when we use it not as a petition but as a supplication that we may become more like Him. Prayer should be regarded as practice of the presence of God. An old peasant was seated alone in the last pew of the village church. 'What are you waiting for?' he was asked; and he answered, 'I am looking at Him and He is looking at me.' Man prays not only that God should remember him, but also that he should remember God.

"How can prayer be defined? Prayer is the effort of man to reach God, to commune with an invisible being, creator of all things, supreme wisdom, truth, beauty, and strength, father, and redeemer of each man. This goal of prayer always remains hidden to intelligence. For both language and thought fail when we attempt to describe God.

"We do know, however, that whenever we address God in fervent prayer we change both soul and body for the better. It could not happen that any man or woman could pray for a single moment without some good result. 'No man ever prayed,' said Emerson, 'without learning something.'

Where To Pray

"One can pray everywhere. In the streets, the subway, the office, the shop, the school, as well as in the solitude of one's own room or among the crowd in a church. There is no prescribed posture, time, or place.

" 'Think of God more often than you breathe,' said

187

Epictetus the Stoic. In order really to mold personality, prayer must become a habit. It is meaningless to pray in the morning and to live like a barbarian the remainder of the day. True prayer is a way of life; the truest life is literally a way of prayer.

"The best prayers are like the improvisations of gifted lovers, always about the same thing yet never twice the same. We cannot all be as creative in prayer as St. Theresa or Bernard of Clairvaux, both of whom poured their adoration into words of mystical beauty. Fortunately, we do not need their eloquence; our slightest impulse to prayer is recognized by God. Even if we are pitifully dumb, or if our tongues are overlaid with vanity or deceit, our meager syllables of praise are acceptable to Him, and He showers us with strengthening manifestations of His love.

"Today as never before prayer is a binding necessity in the lives of men and nations. The lack of emphasis on the religious sense has brought the world to the edge of destruction. Our deepest source of power and perfection has been left miserably undeveloped. Prayer, the basic exercise of the spirit, must be actively practiced in our private lives. The neglected soul of man must be made strong enough to assert itself once more. *For if the power of prayer is again released and used in the lives of common men and women; if the spirit declares its aims clearly and boldly, there is yet hope that our prayers for a better world will be answered.*"

Channing Pollock, the author and playwright, who knew this profound mystery of all mysteries the most profound, but to all men revealed if they will but "ask," had the principal character of his greatest play *The Fool* answer, "If you believe *hard enough*," when the crippled child wanted to know whether prayer would take away her crutches. She prayed and was healed.

Alexis Carrel suggests and he himself believed that "in the lives of common men and women; if the spirit declares its aims clearly and boldly," the better world, the warless world, the world of enduring Peace will be born. That would be the miracle of all miracles, the miracle of the ages.

Many of the commanding civilian and military figures of World War II practiced prayer and believed in a Providence who at last controlled the event, or dictated its final outcome. Some of these leaders were personally devout; others knew only the forms and symbols of their worship. But the one man who was most childlike in his faith and constant in his personal devotions was, at times, the most childish in his actions. General George S. Patton, Jr., recognized as supreme among all tank commanders, was the most profane man I have ever known, either in or out of the Army—and I grew up in the rugged West among lumbermen, where "men were men" with vocabularies accordingly. When he was in the mood, which was generally, Patton used all the words with a few of his own added. How do I explain the paradox? I don't! Here is another of these questions I have "hung up." But General Patton was sincere in his religious practices and he believed in God and loved the Lord—*that I do not doubt*.

Once when an Army chaplain wrote him a man's letter protesting the General's language at a Paris conference called by Patton where women as well as men were present (George Patton believed in equality!), the General replied with an abject apology in which he said essentially this: "I do not know why I do it. Chiefly I regret my language because you and others must believe me insincere when I say that I could not remain in my position for a day were it not for prayer and my faith in God!" He went on to say that he had spent much of the preceding Sunday afternoon in writing his own commentary on the 91st Psalm.

In the spring of 1945 I was in Luxemburg shortly after Bastogne and the reduction of the Bulge. From Chaplain (Col.) James O'Neil, one of the finest chaplains and truest Christians in the service, I received his personal copy of Patton's much discussed prayer, not for rain, but for the rain to stop—the Patton prayer for battle weather.

The circumstances surrounding the writing of that prayer were characteristic. O'Neil, the Third Army Senior Chaplain, was called to Headquarters, and with all the General's characteristic "fervor," ordered to write and circulate a prayer for a cessation of the rains that had reduced visibility to zero, made aerial observation of enemy movements impossible, and generally threatened the entire Third Army front. "Jimmy" O'Neil obeyed orders. A quarter of a million copies of the prayer were circulated and Army presses ran day and night to get out the little cards with the prayer on one side and George S. Patton's Christmas greetings to his soldiers on the other. An attractive card it is. Every man in the Third Army's active theater had one, and I have carried mine ever since. The prayer reads:

"Almighty and most merciful Father, we humbly beseech Thee, of Thy great goodness, restrain these immoderate rains with which we have had to contend. Grant us fair weather for battle. Graciously hearken to us as soldiers who call upon Thee, that armed with Thy power, we may advance from victory to victory and crush the opposition and wickedness of our enemies, and establish Thy justice among men and nations. Amen."

The General's greeting read:

"To each officer and soldier in the Third United States Army I wish a Merry Christmas. I have full confidence in your courage, dedication to duty, and skill in battle. We march in our might to complete victory. May God's blessing rest upon each of you on this Christmas Day.

(signed) G. S. Patton, Jr.
Lieutenant General
Commanding Third United States Army"

That prayer and greeting were typically Patton. They were from the Old Testament rather than the New and had the ring of Joshua and David at their militant best. They were not written for a soft time but for their occasion; they were words to make men strong—and they did.

I wrote from Luxemburg that at home we may no longer believe that God sends rain in answer to prayer; but that along the Rhine I found 250,000 men who believed—firmly believed—that God stopped the rain in answer to their prayers. Everywhere I went, men told me the story and showed me the cards. The only doubters seemed to be among the officers, especially a few chap-plains; but there were no doubters at Patton's head-quarters!

At any rate the rains stopped. They began to subside the morning after that prayer went to press on the evening before. "Battle weather" came and stayed for an unprecedented ten days, during which General Patton's army swept the enemy back to the river and presently beyond.

The Patton Prayer is history now and has in this book only the place of history, but something strangely impressive for me inheres in the incident as it relates to a remarkable human I shall not fully understand until I meet him again, just around the corner. A former member of his staff whom I saw in an old barracks camp in England said, "When he gets to the Gate, if there is any delay, St. Peter will get the shock of his long career—but don't worry, George will go through!"

One of the famous surgeons of the generation immediately following World War I, and the only officer of the Army Medical Corps given the rank of Brigadier General in World War I, Dr. J. M. T. Finney of Johns Hopkins University, made one of his last public appearances at the Russell H. Conwell Breakfast Club in Philadelphia. Among those present were deans of medical colleges, as well as other outstanding scientists in their respective fields. Dr. Finney said that he had never felt justified in entering the operating room without first consulting "The Great Physician." For many years, and at the time of his death, Dr. Finney was an elder in the Brown Memorial Presbyterian Church of Baltimore, Maryland.

I have an intimate friend who ranks among the foremost surgeons of the world in the field of brain surgery, and whose name has been associated with some of the most significant approaches to the ultimate discovery of the cure of cancer, whose spiritual insight approaches that of a seer, whose simple confession of faith, when told to a group of men, is one of the most dramatic stories I have ever heard. He and others of his character and achievement are among the modern miracle workers.

In the sermon of another friend, preached the Sunday before Christmas in the year of this book's writing, I was reminded that 150 years ago the faces of 75 per cent of an audience such as ours would have been disfigured by the scars of smallpox. Which is the greater miracle, the healing of one person in a special crisis by miraculous and Divine intervention, or the wiping out of a plague, the saving of millions, through scientific research and discovery—God, working through men and women to save their fellows?

It was Jesus who said to his disciples—Jesus, the greatest of all miracle workers—"Greater things than these shall ye do. . . ."

Across a deep valley in New Hampshire, on a hilltop one mile away, is an ancient white house facing ours. My friend, who was a medical missionary in Korea and a medical Colonel in World War II, summers there with his family, and presently it will become his permanent home. Already he is one of the half-dozen recognized authorities in his field of medicine. Under God I owe my life to him and his vital Christian faith. His life of prayer matches his scientific knowledge and skill.

193

In Philadelphia is a wise man of another school, a great discoverer in a field practically unexplored before he came upon it by a path of personal pain and sacrifice. I have watched miracles of physical relief and restoration grow under his inspired hands, and my family and my friends have known his healing touch. His genius is half-spiritual at least. He practices the Presence.

"Ask and it shall be given you," is a promise not limited to a particular creed or clan. The Creator is greater than the created and God's ways "are past finding out." God has miracles for Mohammedans and Jews and Christians. And anthropologists testify that "mysteries" appear in the jungles among "pagan peoples."

That last does not excuse me from the practice of His Presence and from "working out my salvation" in the fullness of the light that has shone upon me.

The supreme demonstration of united prayer, of corporate petition and supplication that I have seen and experienced, is the Wailing Wall at the foundations of the ancient Temple in Jerusalem. For two thousand years the Jews have wept here. For two thousand years they have confessed their sins and claimed the fulfillment of the Prophecies. Here, for two thousand years, they have triumphantly proclaimed "The Return" and the rebuilding of Zion.

Once when I came to that sacred wall and heard the weeping and lamenting worshippers, I was caught up by a strange ecstasy. It seemed that the foundations were moved, that the world rocked and that the Heavens opened.

194

Who shall say that two thousand years of prayers have not been answered in the return to Palestine and in the creation of modern Israel?

God grant that prayer shall become now, for this new nation, the way to Peace with Power.

XXV

The Road of Unity to Power

ONLY a Christlike world will ever be a world of peace, and only Christlike men and women will ever build a permanent security from the threat of war. It is as simple as that and, of course, as difficult.

Nearly one-half of America—approximately seventy million people—belongs to no religious group: Catholic, Protestant, Jewish, or any of the smaller sects. Indifference, not intolerance, is the major problem of religion in the United States today. Recently a secular writer declared: "This country faces three alternatives—Protestantism, Roman Catholicism, or paganism," and he affirmed that either of the first two was infinitely to be preferred to the last. . . . I propose a fourth—Christianity.

Christianity is first of all a faith, not an institution or even a way of life. It is a belief; and if ever again Christians believe hard enough, they may accomplish in their

197

time a world revolution as complete as that which followed the conversion of the Roman Emperor Constantine in the fourth century.

But Christianity is not just any faith. What you believe does make a difference, and it is here that the genius and uniqueness of Christianity lie. Christianity is faith in Jesus Christ as the Son of God. Theologically that faith is expressed in the phrase "very God of very God" or, as the Apostles' Creed has it, "Jesus Christ his only Son our Lord," and the issue is the deity of Jesus. Dostoievski in *The Possessed* made one of his characters say that Christianity turns on one question and one alone: "Whether a man as a civilized being . . . can believe at all, believe, that is, in the Divinity of the Son of God, Jesus Christ, for therein rests, strictly speaking, the whole faith."

But when, as in some of the so-called Christian churches today, Jesus Christ is stripped of His deity and becomes just "a good man," however great, He is left with less moral authority than Abraham Lincoln or Leo Tolstoy, and infinitely less than Buddha or Confucius.

I am a Protestant who passionately holds to his tradition and to the theological particulars of Protestantism. But I now face squarely the fact that the unity of Roman Catholicism on the deity of Jesus puts me both in debt and in shame. Let us not blink the fact that in this regard the Roman Catholic Church has a faith that challenges the Protestant churches and cuts across the Protestant tradition of freedom. As a Protestant, I agree that under the American Constitution the Roman Catholic Church has full right to propagate and proselytize for the Catholic faith, full right to win America to its belief—and the Roman Catholic Church is not bigoted when it does so. Equally under the Constitution, the Protestant Churches have this same right—no more, and no less. Specifically and finally, they do not accept the authoritarian Roman Catholic position, and they are not bigots when they reject it and strive to support, strengthen, and unify their own faith. The bigot is that low fellow who refuses to another what he claims for himself and who is forever shouting "bigot." But there is something in common beyond the particulars of each faith, something immediate and imperative to all Christians—our responsibility for the spiritual defenses of the nation and for unyielding progress toward an enduring world peace. In this atomic age the ultimatum presented to civilization is Christ or chaos, and Christians of whatever name or sign must be Christians first and always.

Happily, within Protestantism today I see and feel a rising tide of return to Jesus Christ as "very God," for Jesus Christ alone accomplishes the new birth within me, redeems me and, through me, redeems the little world in which I move. And here is the only formula that will save mankind.

If the irreducible minimum of Christianity is faithful acceptance of Jesus Christ as the Son of God, then specifically what does that mean to me? To me it means an experience. There are many particulars of my faith which I accept intellectually, but which are not within the realm of my experience—for instance, the virgin birth. But I believe in immortality, in eternal life, because it has been a personal experience for me ever since a Febru-

ary morning in 1918 out in front of Toul in France—
an experience which is already a story within this story.

And equally to me, as I have already written, "the
Deity of Jesus Christ has become like that experience
in front of Toul. To me He is God, my experience; and
without Him I would have no God."

The Protestant Reformation in none of its parts or particulars and never in the personal faith of its leaders—
Luther, Calvin, Knox, and the earlier Valdez, and all
their contemporaries—questioned the Deity of Jesus or
ever conceded freedom to question. That "freedom,"
wherever exercised, was taken later, but never resulted
in any considerable withdrawals and has never achieved
numerical power.

The uniqueness of His Person, His Passion, the fact
that He is "very God of very God," is held as unequiv-
ocally by the Reformation as by the Roman Catholic
Church.

This unity of Protestant faith is another thing altogether than the organic union of Protestant Churches or
even their constantly strengthening unity in program and
action.

But "the faith once delivered," loyalty to it, unequiv-
ocating orthodoxy, is definitely not enough. By all the
tests of the law, the Pharisee who despised the Publican
was "orthodox." In his religious practices David was
orthodox even in the evil day when he took Uriah's
wife and became responsible for the death of his brave
captain. The Inquisitors in Spain and South America
were superlative in their orthodoxy, as were the witch
hangers in early New England. These and many others

THE ROAD OF UNITY TO POWER

equally inhuman were punctilious keepers of the naked tenets of the Faith. They found the "authority" for all the tortures they inflicted upon their hapless fellow humans.

Today their kind continues and the Inquisitors, the witch hangers of this tragic and unchristianlike succession, write and preach to consign to "outer darkness" and worse those who do not shout their shibboleths or conform to their interpretations. Jesus said let the wheat and tares grow together until the harvest (and he, at last, is both the Judge and Harvester) lest in rooting out the weeds, good grain is also destroyed. But too many of us pound ourselves on the chest, insist that ours is the way, the truth, and the life, and advance the harvest date to suit our particular "threshing" style and calendar.

A severe and dogmatic woman was finally persuaded to hear one of the most distinguished clergymen of our time. She had a deep prejudice against the man. Things she had seen and heard about him and sentences she had read from his pen had convinced her that he was not "orthodox." But after hearing him through a pre-Easter week of profoundly moving addresses, she remarked in a burst of spontaneous enthusiasm, "He is wonderful! So Christlike!" And then resuming her former prejudices, she shook her head and added, "Too bad he isn't orthodox."

Yes, definitely there is something more required than that I shall be "letter perfect" in my intellectual acceptance of an recital of the creed. Orthodoxy is not enough, for as St. Paul said, and as I write again into this book: "He hath made us able ministers of the New

Testament. Not of the letter but of the spirit, for the letter killeth, but the spirit giveth Life."

Beyond my Reformation heritage is the imperative of the present unpredictable hour in human history. Catholics, Jews, Protestants—all believers in God must unite to present an unbroken front and the maximum of Power in the face of a militant and united atheism.

In this book we have returned again and again to the four *Dorchester* chaplains of the three faiths, and again we return:

Each had a dynamic loyalty to his particular faith. To each his vows of ordination were holy, and they were passionately held. Nowhere in America could four men be found more intense in their devotion to their own faiths. But these four became one in service, in sacrifice, and in dying. Standing shoulder to shoulder, their arms linked, and braced against the rail as the waters rose about them, each in the tradition of his faith prayed to God the Father of us all. Each was loyal to himself, but each had found a cause transcending all differences and divisions, even as their deed transcends all debate and arguments.

It was this unity that won the war.

But there are defeatists among us who insist that we did not win the war, and certainly a case can be made for their contention. They point to ruined cities, nations in rubble, disintegrating cultures, and the prospect of an atomic war to complete the universal ruin. They say, "The world, including us, is worse off now, and steadily so, than it was before and after World War I."

Some time ago I flew from Amsterdam to London with a decorated R.A.F. pilot who was now flying with the Dutch. When we were well over the water, he came back and knelt in the narrow aisle by my chair. In the course of the conversation he said, "Sir, Hitler was right! It was the only decent thing he ever said. You remember? Back in 1940 he declared that no nation would win the war. That all would lose. Believe me, we have!"

I nodded in assent and replied, "Yes, I understand. But there is a difference, and this difference is—or may become—everything. We won the chance, the fighting chance, to *win* the *Peace*. That, I say, is *everything*."

Winning the war and winning the Peace are one. If we fail to win the Peace, then indeed we have lost the war and "these Dead" have died in vain. Please God they shall not die in vain!

Unity won the war and less than unity will lose the Peace. Beyond this our unity at home, American unity, *not uniformity,* but all races, faiths, and colors living and working together, practicing man's brotherhood in God's fatherhood is the first, and indeed the irreducible, minimum of our worthy contribution toward an enduring world Peace.

Flying in from Dakar on the East African Coast, I arrived in Natal, Brazil, one April afternoon in 1943. In the senior chaplain of that great base I found an old friend. He was a Protestant and his associate was a Roman Catholic. I had broken the wristband on my watch and suggested that the chaplain take me to the city for a replacement. He grinned, but shook his head.

"Sorry, but this is Friday and tonight I am conducting the Jewish service for Father Ryan!" he said.

I looked my amazement and he explained that there were seventy-two Jewish boys on the Base but no resident Rabbi, no Jewish chaplain. The two Christian chaplains had organized the Jewish service of worship and, at the appointed time each Friday evening, and each in his turn, the Catholic and Protestant chaplains brought the spiritual message. "This was Father Ryan's day," said my friend, "but he is ill and I am taking his place."

Well I was no longer interested in my wristband and I didn't go to the city of Natal. I remained right there and saw Sam Overstreet, a Baptist preacher from New England, conduct a Jewish service for a Roman Catholic priest.

In war chapels all over the world I saw men of every faith, at their appointed time, worship under the same roof, and I listened while clergymen of the three faiths officiated before the same altar, suitably dressed for each occasion. There were times when Protestant and Jewish boys died in the arms of their Catholic chaplains and other times when Protestant and Jewish chaplains gave a modified form of the last rites of the Roman Catholic Church to members of that faith. This was unity without uniformity.

I do not ask, nor ever suggest, that the particulars of this wartime unity be brought into the Peace. That would be quite unreasonable. But I do write here that if we fail to carry into the Peace, into our peacetime relationships, the spirit of that Unity—indeed, if we fail to strengthen our peacetime unity, then we shall lose the Peace.

Our greatest danger, our most challenging foe, is not without, but within!

The Religion in Life group in Philadelphia is an interfaith organization of women with an honored history of more than a decade. Shortly after the surrender was signed on the deck of the battleship *Missouri* in the Far East, this organization held an interfaith meeting in the club rooms of historic Christ Church. I presided that night and introduced three speakers, one from each faith.

An eloquent young Jew, a lieutenant commander in the Navy, who was completing his law course at the University of Pennsylvania, spoke first. He was followed by a Protestant chaplain convalescing from war wounds in the Valley Forge General Hospital at Phoenixville, Pennsylvania. The final speaker, a Roman Catholic, was a G.I. student in Villanova College. Because of late classes, he arrived during the program and while the chaplain was talking. Standing in the rear of the room, he waited until the chaplain had finished, and then hurried to the platform. He pushed by my extended hand and when with some surprise I turned to follow him, I saw that the chaplain was greeting him in a deeply moving reunion.

Later the young Catholic said, "The last time I saw the chaplain, he was looking down at me and I was looking up at him from a stretcher on Utah beach. He had lifted me to that stretcher. Later he helped lift me into an ambulance and then a little later he got his." The young man continued, "In those days we never asked are there Catholics on our left or Jews or our right or Protestants in support. We were just Americans!" He concluded then, "And we must be like that now!"

To win the Peace, *"we must be like that now."*

As to our own Protestant heritage and mission, we have been busy about many things and all of them important, I am sure, but we have forgotten that which is first and, in forgetting that, to this hour, we have lost the Peace. We have organized the ecumenical movement, we have united many Protestant denominations, we have gone about Christianizing the social order, each after his own pattern and plan. We have debated doctrine and liturgical forms, and we have advised and even condemned the statesmen. Indeed we churchmen have had as many formulas for peace and world security as there are sects among us. But Jesus stands at the door and knocks, and we are talking so loudly that we cannot hear Him. "Behold, I will make all things new," He is saying, and He will do just that if we let Him in and then go out with Him, as did Peter and Paul and the rest, out to the ends of the earth and to the last extremities of man.

The Wesley revival of the eighteenth century saved England from the horrors of the French Revolution and accomplished an even greater social revolt in Britain. That revival began in the soul of John Wesley himself after his "heart-warming experience" in Aldersgate Street. The spiritual equivalent of that revival now, on a world scale, would be even more potent than the Marshall Plan or a Pacific Pact, both of which I support. Without bloodshed, it would save the world from Communism.

Bishop Fred Fisher once said: "It is not the business of Christianity to provide an organization for the world but to infuse the spirit of Christ into the organizations of the world."

What then must a man, a nation, or a civilization do to become, to be Christian?

First, the uniqueness of Jesus, His deity, must be acknowledged. The world has gone to the end of the trail with every other person, every other plan, every other program, and has come upon disasters that have all but wrecked man. Man wants now the final word and an adequate leader. A half-god will not do. A materialistic theology has watered down the divinity of Jesus until, if it prevails further, adequate authority and power will be drained from a so-called Christianity.

Second, what Jesus has to say must be accepted as practical and imperative here and now. The indifferent community giving Him a certain intellectual obeisance has brushed Him off as an impractical visionary. But even more tragic, many churches and churchmen have gone right along with the community, so that the conflict between Sunday worship and workday practices has steadily increased. Charles M. Sheldon once wrote a novel with the title *In His Steps: What Would Jesus Do?* It is hardly as simple as that, for even if I knew specifically what Jesus would do in a particular situation, I could not do it. I am not Jesus. But I may become what the Pacific Islander who had been Christianized described himself as being—"a Jesus man." It is not "What would Jesus do?" but "What would Jesus have me do?" and always I may find the answer to that question.

Individuals who have put the Christian ethic to work in their lives and in their business affairs have demonstrated success. We cite the Quakers of Pennsylvania. Certainly they are an example. But equally effective was the application of the Christian ethic by the Pilgrims in New England, Roger Williams in Rhode Island, the Catholics in Maryland, and the Dutch in New Amsterdam when they received the Jews from Brazil.

Jesus Christ has the answer, is the answer, for the individual, for the community, for the state, for the world. A Christlike world would be a world at peace. Even as He accomplishes within the individual the great redemption, He redeems society through redeemed individuals.

The greater miracle is not the instantaneous cure of an "incurable" disease. It is the new birth of which Jesus spoke to Nicodemus, the ruler of the Synagogue, when he said, "Ye must be born again." Not a physical birth, but a spiritual birth; and not for time alone, but for eternity.

On Christmas Sunday, 1949, Dr. Norman Vincent Peale related the following incident in his morning sermon. "Six years ago a man came into this church utterly defeated. He was a man of fine education and attainments, brilliant in mind, but he was an alcoholic and his was one of the worst cases I ever knew. He had been discharged three times from a very important position, and his employer had said, 'Now it is the end.'

"He was hopeless, completely hopeless. But I said to him, 'If you will accept Jesus Christ, that is, if you will turn to Him in your mind by faith and believe that He can do this for you, He will lift you above your defeat. He will change you.'

"He believed and surrendered to the Master and one night in this church sitting in the fourth seat from the front, Jesus Christ touched him and he was changed. His associates and physicians said to me, 'This is incredible.'

"Here is the letter from the man himself. He writes me every year at just about this time: 'Well, early December will soon be with us again. That will be the sixth anniversary of my rebirth, my turning back to God and my family. My gratitude to God is boundless. It thrills me to write it again. I do not need to mention my old trouble —now six years dead. It is gone and done forever. But the absolute and complete ease with which it finally came about minus even a single temptation or struggle is one of God's miracles and the constant proof of the grace and mercy of God.'

"The man who writes this letter is one of the heads of his industry, one of the keenest men in his field in American business today."

This is the birth, the miracle that in a man's mental and physical maturity brings him to moral and spiritual maturity, redeems and perfects his soul beyond every possible physical imperfection. There is a sure sign that this miracle has been performed—the gratitude of those who experience it and their love for and adoration of the One who performs it.

How this "redemption" operates in men, and how it changes them without regard to their social status or previous economic level, is demonstrated day after day where I may and do witness the change, in the old Mission on the Bowery. These men are all about me in the various enterprises of our association. From the gutter, from that street of "no return," and from prison they have come confessing their sins, seeking and finding their Redeemer. Now rehabilitated, they are, and have been for years, respected in their communities and constructive members of society.

Here is the process of redemption, the method of the Master in that highest of all arts, and the genius of His Gospel. Here is the practical power of salvation for the world. And as for the individual, so for society (which is but the unity made up of individuals) prayer is the road to Peace with Power.

Do you say, "It is too slow." Well, we have tried the swifter offerings. We have tried them all and now we have come to the atomic answer—the answer that may wreck man.

Here it is well to remember what Dr. Carrel concludes: ". . . If the power of prayer is again released and used in the lives of common men and women; if the spirit declares its aims clearly and boldly, there is yet hope that our prayers for a better world will be answered."

The alternative is death for man.

Third, the ideal must be put to work and the spirit must come alive in deeds. Faith in Christ as God must become a veritable passion in those who determine now, at whatever cost, to follow Him. And in that faith we must go steadily about the business of answering our own prayers!

In July, 1934, I was in Berlin and heard Hitler attempt to explain his "blood purge." It was a night of terror. Following that "unspeakable" speech, I walked with two young friends under the lindens. They were members of the German Christian Endeavor Union, a youth program that throughout the Hitler period remained adamant in its refusal to become Nazi. During the preceding week the executive committee of this group had met in Berlin and adopted resolutions that under the circumstances were prophetic. They declared themselves loyal to the fatherland, ready to die in its defense, but they disagreed with the so-called Aryan clause, which would lift one race above all other races. They said, "To this we do not consent. It is not Christian." And finally the resolutions closed with these heroic words: "At whatever cost we choose Christ."

One of the two men with whom I walked that night was a University of Leipzig graduate who had been my interpreter on two previous visits to Germany. He explained the resolutions in detail, insisting that there was evidence that the Fuhrer was moving steadily toward moderation, that having won his leadership he would now administer it without fanaticism, and that presently all would be well. But I insisted on an answer to my question: "If presently all is not well, if this Aryan clause is made the test, if the pattern boldly outlined in *Mein Kampf* becomes Germany's policy, then what?" And then came the fateful answer: "Then, sir, at whatever cost, we choose Christ."

Though we cannot conceive of such a moral crisis ever arising in America, the crisis itself is beyond doctrinaire pacifism. These German youths were not pacifists. They were Christians, and not even for their country would they fight in a cause they believed to be anti-

Christian. God forbid that ever in America, Christian youth should be faced with that decision.

The next day I left Berlin. I never saw my friend again. He died in a concentration camp, as did many of his associates. They saw it through, they kept their faith and, choosing Christ, followed Him to the death. Now, throughout Germany, their comrades, young men and young women, are putting their lives into the foundations of a new and democratic nation.

In July, 1946, I was flying back to the United States from Scotland by way of Iceland and the tip of Greenland. Shortly after the take-off from Reykjavik the captain of the plane came to me with a map and, pointing to a cross off Greenland, he said, "It marks the *Dorchester.* When we reach that spot, we shall circle and dip and you will know." But as we approached Greenland, fog came down and the ocean was blotted out. Under the sun and above another white and shoreless sea, we flew high above the North Atlantic. I was glad. It seemed altogether fitting that time and space, their oceans and their controversies, and the transport with the heroes it entombed should all be covered. The captain returned and said, "I am sorry, sir, but we shall circle and dip."

Presently the great ship lifted, then circled and dove into the fog. Twice she circled above the dark and faceless water, and then flinging the fog and mist from her mighty wings, she rose like a homing eagle into the sun. And there was light everywhere.

"I am the light of the world," Jesus said. "Ask and it shall be given you."

Faith is power—for you.

APPENDIX

THE UNITED STATES OF AMERICA

To all who shall see these presents, greeting:

This is to certify that

The President of the United States of America
in accordance with the order issued by General
George Washington at Headquarters, Newburgh,
New York, on August 7, 1782, and pursuant to act
of Congress, has awarded the Medal

FOR MERIT

to

DR. DANIEL ALFRED POLING

*For extraordinary fidelity and exceptionally
meritorious conduct*

Given under my hand in the City of Washington
this 29th day of March, 1947

Dean Acheson /S/
Acting Secretary of State

/S/ Harry Truman
Commander-in-Chief

The

WAR DEPARTMENT

expresses its appreciation for

patriotic service to

DANIEL A. POLING

For outstanding and conspicuous service as an accredited war correspondent serving with our armed forces in an overseas theater of combat.

Washington, D. C.
23 November 1946

Robert P. Patterson
Secretary of War

May 15, 1944

Dear Doctor Poling:

Your selection by the churches of America as their representative to the churches of Australia and Australia's hearty invitation extended to you, make you, in these significant days, your country's spiritual ambassador of good will.

Your mission will carry great weight from the fact that you will represent the Federal Council of Churches of Christ in America; the World's Alliance for International Friendship through the Churches; the Christian Peace Union; the World's Christian Endeavor Union and the American and Foreign Christian Union. You will thus become the voice of millions of your American fellow Christians.

Coming at this critical time in the history of nations when the peoples of Australia and of the United States are so closely identified in a common great cause, this visit from one in your high position in the religious and cultural life of America is of immense significance. I believe that it will add moral value to all official contacts between our two countries.

You have made other notable journeys for the church and for your country, but this mission to Australia presents you with perhaps your greatest opportunity, the opportunity to interpret the spiritual ideals of America to religious leaders and citizens of Australia upon whose friendship and cooperation now, and in the postwar world, so much of future peace and security in the Pacific will depend.

To you the war is not remote, for your son, Chaplain Clark V. Poling, has made the supreme sacrifice—this fact will bring you close to the heart of a great people that has given greatly to our common cause.

The prayers of your fellow Americans will accompany you.

Very sincerely yours,

/S/ FRANKLIN D. ROOSEVELT

Rev. Dr. Daniel A. Poling,
c/o The Christian Herald,
419 Fourth Avenue,
New York, New York.

264.1 Po
POLING, DANIEL A.
Faith is Power For You

264.1 Po
POLING, DANIEL A.
Faith is Power For You